What they say about
THE CHRONICLES C

Reading Peppy's book hurt 1.

uncompromising, so well-written. All those who dabble in the quick-fix mode of ministry should read this book and learn. Peppy has been obedient to God in writing her book, but the stumbling and the slipping and the getting up again and her sheer persistence all bear witness to the cost of doing what she is told. Thank God for her loving family. Thank God for her caring friends. Thank God for God. The journey continues, but she is not alone.

Adrian Plass, best-selling author and speaker

For those of us who have suffered abuse, one of the greatest challenges is to have the courage to break out of hiding and to tell our stories. Until we do, we live perpetually in the dismal half-light of mere survival. This is why *The Chronicles of the Box* is an important book for all who seek freedom from toxic shame. In it, Peppy Ulyett bravely and transparently describes her recovery from the trauma of abuse. Using entries from her journal, Peppy invites us into her story and to travel with her from the Good Friday of degradation to the Easter Day of restoration. Isn't it time you left your tomb behind?

Dr Mark Stibbe, best-selling author and abuse survivor

We are healed and we are being healed and we will be healed. Healing is not an event but a journey. Peppy's story shows her as vulnerable, honest, and hopeful – even in the dark. It's a messy, untidy, but powerful account. Many people who are still making progress in their healing are tempted to think it's a worthless journey, and they will be enormously helped by Peppy's candour.

Russ Parker – Founder and Director of 2Restore: Healing Church Wounds; author of Healing Wounded History

I am profoundly struck by the unflinching bravery and persistent pursuing of healing demonstrated by Peppy. This is a sensitively-wrought account of an awesome journey and a deep encouragement to any of us on long, complex voyages of restoration. It is a wake-up call to the Church that the subject of sexual abuse is not to be ignored, to not limit God nor fear such a hidden wound coming into the light. An inspirational read!

Sara Hyde, Criminal Justice Support Worker, Vice Chair of the Women's Fabian Society

The Chronicles of the Box

A personal journey of healing and restoration from shame

by Peppy Ulyett with Lin Ball

'...like Jesus, he who proclaims liberation is called not only to care for his own wounds and the wounds of others, but also to make his wounds into a major source of his healing power.'

Henri Nouwen *Wounded Healer*

21 20 19 18 17 7 6 5 4 3 2 1

First published 2017 by Malcolm Down Publishing Ltd.
www.malcolmdown.co.uk

British Library Cataloguing in Publication Data: a catalogue record for this book is available from the British Library.

ISBN 978-1-910786-69-7

Cover illustration by Gill Pedler
Cover design and internal layout by John Ball

Printed in the UK

For all those who wander with woundedness,
and wonder about God.

With thanks to my two 'companions on the way';
also, I have enormous gratitude to Lin and John for their
dedication and unwavering support in getting this story published;
to Bill and Gary for their faithfulness, encouragement and
wisdom; to Janice for her steadfast care;
most of all to my marvellous husband and children, who
have shown such acceptance and love throughout.
I am so thankful to you all.

About this book

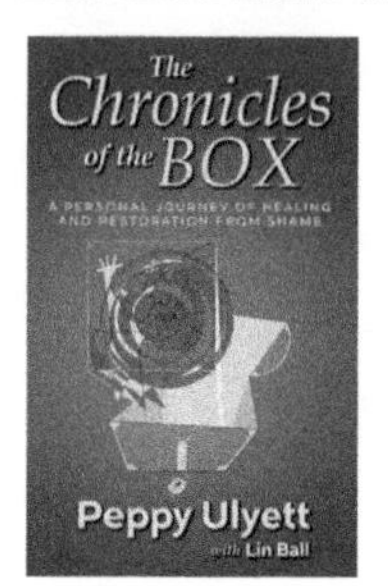

The effects of past abuse were threatening to blow the lid off the box of Peppy Ulyett's life. But a loving and powerful God helped her unpack its shameful hoard, releasing her from the tyranny of silence.

This is a story of restoration from shame and its toxic effects. Peppy invites you to journey with her through her journal entries and emails as she discovers astonishing healing from God.

In the journey to healing, Peppy reached a major turning point where she was able to pray sincerely for the men who had abused her, and really know what it was to forgive them.

This book is not an easy read, especially if you too have been abused, but within its pages you may find the hope and courage to work your way towards the sort of healing and reconciliations Peppy finally experienced.

About the author

Peppy Ulyett has stumbled her fringe and frabjous way to middle-age in the middle of England, despite life's circumstances and her complicated character. This is because she has a God who loves her and wants the best for her, whether she's comfortable with it or not. She's enormously grateful for all of that.

Peppy – trained listener, carer, amateur puppeteer, night-shelter volunteer and church worker – blogs at **peppyulyett.wordpress.com**

An invitation

This is my story of restoration from shame and its toxic effects. I invite you to journey with me through my journal entries and emails as I discover astonishing healing from God. The effects of past abuse were threatening to blow the lid off the box of my life. But a loving and powerful God helped me unpack its shameful hoard, releasing me from the tyranny of silence. I understood that it was a story to be shared, to show how God is in the mess of life and wants to work with each of us to free us, redeeming the hurt and shame, giving dignity.

All individuals are unique and their stories are particular to them. But I believe that the themes of my story can be shared and used by others.

My story is painful, so why am I telling it so publicly?

In the journey to healing, I reached a major turning point where I was able to pray sincerely for the two men who had abused me, and really know what it was to forgive them.

Of course, forgiveness doesn't happen at one isolated point in time. I've had to return to it privately, time and time again. I've been helped in this by the online *Forgiveness Challenge* put together by Bishop Desmond Tutu and his daughter Mpho (**www.humanjourney.com/forgiveness/**).

Part of that journey has also been to forgive my mother, who seems likely to have been a knowing bystander to my abuse as a child. It has taken time, but I am now at ease with her. It will probably not become a very warm or close relationship. She remains emotionally distant to me. But I'm at peace with that. I have let it go.

I've even returned to the town where it all happened. I spent a couple of hours walking around, facing the memories. It felt hard and unsettling but was still cathartic.

I know that there will still be challenges. Situations will arise which will threaten to take me back into the pain. But God has shown me that he is taking care of this. I just have to deal with things as they come up. I don't need to have all the answers – because he does.

I'm aware that this book isn't an easy read, and it will be harder if you too have been abused. It's been very costly to write. It can't be read lightly. It's raw because I've re-lived much in the writing. A great deal of the text is drawn from unedited emails written when I was at the end of myself, at the end of my resources, desperate. My promise to you is that it's all true, although some names have been changed.

This outline may help you:

- **Part 1** of *The Chronicles of the Box* covers a year – what I originally thought was to be the whole story of God healing me. God was teaching me to trust him with my fears and shame.
- **Part 2** relates to the following year, when deeper, hidden levels of shame overwhelmed me and God healed again. It deals with how I met and dealt with the overwhelming sense of threat and terror about breaking my silence and 'telling'.
- **Part 3** is the follow-up story – a time of recovery and growing ministry; and some hard setbacks.
- **Part 4** provides a kind of epilogue and some thoughts from those most closely involved.

By the way, some people are confused when first picking up the book about whether I'm Penny or Peppy. Don't worry… all will be become plain!

The Chronicles of the Box

Part 1

1: Awake

Journal extracts – January to February of Year 1

I'm always the first awake. Daisie greets my descent downstairs with a nuzzle of her face round the edge of her bed and an offering of her belly for gentle rubbing as I enter the kitchen. She sighs deeply as I cross to the kettle, a half-milk coffee with a spoonful of dark brown sugar being the way to indulge and delight my tastebuds after my fingertips.

As the mug of milk turns in the whirring microwave and the kettle's rumbling escalates, I step out into the fresh stillness of the garden.

'Morning, girls,' I murmur. 'Ready for breakfast?'

Befuddled and curious 'oohs' tentatively rise from the henhouse as I lower the ramp and open the door. The hens step and stagger out, shake and ruffle their plumage, then dash after my retreating legs as we all head for the food store. Grain and pellets are greeted with a chorus of cooing, the urgency to begin pecking distracting them from the hand that sweeps down one or two feathery backs.

Back in the kitchen, I savour the warmth and sweetness of the coffee and ponder the day.

I am here waiting for this different day to unfold because of four pictures. Yes, there have been four pictures now. Pictures which are similar, yet with significant differences, that together urge me to move forward by looking back. But what's the point?

Anyway… four pictures.

In the first picture, I am standing on a ladder, half within the attic space, looking in. It's gloomy in there, with no natural light; very dusty and a little bleak. The wall along the left side is all uneven brickwork and rough mortar. The slope of the roof extends quite steeply down to my right. The lines of the rafters stretch away in front of me, converging towards the box lying centrally, towards the rear of this place. The attic is otherwise empty. The box is all that is here. It dominates the space, quietly commanding my attention.

So, to describe the box… It's a wooden box, a small chest; very solidly built, with a domed lid. The reinforcing straps, corner pieces and front lock are of dark metal. There is a heavy padlock fixed through the clasp. The contents are secure within.

I know immediately what it represents; that the box holds pieces of my past. Appropriately contained. My past has not been entirely secret, but the detail has never been for public display.

In the second picture, as I stand on the loft ladder, I am twisting round, looking back over my right shoulder, seeing the box now wedged into the eaves and butted against the back wall. The lock remains fast. Why has it moved? A curious shift, but I do not feel particularly concerned about it.

Then, the third picture. Standing on the ladder, I still have to twist to see the box in the back corner of the attic. But now there is an unsettling change. The lock is undone, the clasp hangs open. It is not completely secure anymore, and neither am I. But I do not need to worry too much, I tell myself. After all, the lid is heavy and sits firmly shut – and only I am here to look on it. I will leave it alone. This time, though, I find the undercurrent of uncertainty and unsettledness does not leave me; it rises and continually ripples the edges of my ease.

What does it all mean? Yes, I know there are events from my past that I have 'put away'. They are behind me now. I have found a good and safe place to be. It's the movement of the box that I puzzle over. It seems that God is showing me that perhaps it shouldn't stay in place. Yet while it is shown to be moveable, I feel there is a degree of restraint being demonstrated too. God has the power to challenge and change its position, though still invites me to engage with what is happening and consent to what is to come. And yet – what is to come?

In the fourth and last picture, I see the box back in its original position, straight in front of me as I lift my head through the hatch into the attic. My stomach lurches as I see the padlock still disjointed, hanging with its neck broken. It is disturbing to view it, even though I note that the lock has not actually been removed, as though that is something left for me to choose to do. There is no mistaking the challenge being pressed upon me, though: 'What are you going to do about the box?'

So, what *am* I going to do about the box?

These pictures are making me uncomfortable, deep in my spirit. I know something of what they relate to, but feel confused by what I am supposed to do about them. I'm nervous of explaining my situation. I have asked John, my church minister, if I can talk to him. He's a dynamic if somewhat disorganised person, and a gifted preacher. I hope he will be relaxed and receptive when I see him. What will he think of my pictures? How will he relate to this unusual way in which I am hearing from God? But I can't easily hold this to myself any longer. I need wise counsel, so here I am, in trusting apprehension.

The pictures have come to me over the course of this last year. Yes, I've always understood what they represented; it's really not hard to work that out. The pictures are all set in the same place, in the same attic. I know which house holds this attic, even though I cannot see the other rooms from the vantage point I have to the pictures. And, in fact, I do not recall ever looking into the attic in that house. Nevertheless, I recognise it, just the same.

So the appointed time arrives, this February 2011 day, and this is how it is. I'm a relative newcomer to this church, known enough to John but not too much. I am the puppeteer and also 'the lady who signs when we sing'. But that tells him nothing about who I used to be. So now I skate through the basic background that John needs to know.

As a young child, I lived abroad with my parents and sisters, as my father worked for the Foreign Office. After a tempestuous few years, my parents divorced when I was about eight. Dad remained living abroad and, although I had sporadic contact with him, I didn't meet up with him again until I was in my mid twenties. Back in England with my mother, a quick remarriage brought a new man into our home. A heavy drinker and bully, he had a known history of inappropriate behaviour with young girls. I became a particular focus of his attentions over several years, in ways which instilled fear and shame in me. I know that the box in the pictures holds that past.

John listens to my description of the pictures and asks whether I have ever 'unpacked' this box before. Yes, I have done so. Once, I explain uncomfortably. A few years ago. Surely, there's no need to do so again? You see, I showed its contents to the police, who carefully and gently picked through it and prepared to lay it open in court – to prevent other boxes needing to be packed away in other attics. But then, the one who made the pieces grubby and torn – the pieces that needed to be contained – was discovered to be no more. The potential for him causing further shameful baggage was at an end. Justice would be dealt perfectly and eternally. The box was re-packed; the lid shut; the door closed. It could be let be.

So there is no need to open this box again. Is there?

'But have you ever unpacked this box before Jesus?' John asks.

I am rocked by his question, shaken by what he is suggesting should be done about the pictures. It makes a kind of sense, but I am dismayed.

'But… but what would be the point?' I ask. 'What is the good purpose in it?'

'Your healing and wholeness,' he says. 'Isn't that enough?'

No! I think. Well… yes, of course. I mean… I can't dismiss or reject God's desire for me to be healed and whole. But I've been fine lately. I'm happy, secure, pretty sorted really. Why pick a scab?

It's not causing me a problem. I can't think of any reason I should need it all re-exposed. No purpose to it. No good purpose at all.

I need to take time to think and pray.

It's a busy month for us, February. Three birthdays in less than a fortnight and half term bisecting the calendar of events. This half term week is particularly hectic, mostly with the chauffeuring and hosting duties that fall to parents of teenagers. On two days I make three one-hour round trips to the hospital for a friend having chemo, whose belligerent optimism is frequently expressed by her phrase, 'I'm fine'. Plus there are two trips for my son George to visit friends who live over ten miles away, and then there's a girlfriend dropping in to see him at home. Meanwhile, my daughter Elly has a friend staying for a couple of nights before they go off to a concert in Birmingham, and another friend here for a sleepover. They go to London on a theatre and sightseeing trip – our birthday present to her – and I pick them up from the station again that evening, then take them to a party in town.

The week's diary means that my husband Michael and I somewhat lack a social life. My big triumph of the week is to get all the ironing done. A rare event indeed!

But, as a backdrop to all this busyness, I am considering the pictures and John's disturbing challenge.

2: Time to unpack

Emails and journal entries – March of Year 1

March 9, 08:19
To: **John**
Subject: **unpacking the box**

John,

I will trust God with the unpacking of the box. He has been speaking to me every day since our chat. I accept what he is saying on this.

Penny

My early morning ponderings today are ushered from my heart by George, my gangling mid-teen, trailing an urgency of appetite in his wake. He is quiet, absorbed in his own drifting thought-life, while my attention is held by the clock as I calculate the risks of him missing the school bus. Older sister Elly flurries through – sometimes amused and sometimes irritated by the routine of chivvying met by resistance and protestation that her mum and brother can't seem to disentangle from. My husband Michael quietly finishes his coffee, seemingly detached from the fray. They all leave the house within minutes of each other, and a pair of expectant eyes call my attention to the next phase of the day – the dog walk.

Oversized trousers and old coat swathe my dishevelled appearance, with a wide brimmed waxed cotton hat shielding sight of my rumpled head. Daisie and I set off along the road outside the house, walking just a few hundred yards until we push through the gap in the spinney on the corner. This is my moment of greeting God, imagining him falling into step alongside me and delighting in the dialogue we may find between us. On a mellow day I might start by simply marvelling at some detail of the created world around me, or by thanking him for being with me. If out of sorts and distracted, I say, 'Almighty God, have mercy on me, and be with me.' That puts his awesome love and grace back into the foreground of my awareness, and gives me a sense of honour at the company I am keeping, from which point I can speak trustingly and honestly to him.

March 11, 13:08
To: **John**
Subject: **unpacking the box**

I'm struggling with 'unpacking the box'. At the moment, a degree of vulnerability has opened up in me which is proving quite hard to manage. I do want you to be part of any prayer ministry to deal with it but, as you said, it will be hard for you to commit to being there much before your 3-month sabbatical. If therefore it needs to wait until later in the year so that you can be available, perhaps I need to pack it all away again until we're ready to face it, and so be more at ease in the meantime? But I find I can't do that, the way things are at the moment...

Penny

March 15, 08:06
To: **John**
Subject: **the box again**

On Sunday I had a difficult time during the morning service. The songs 'What a friend we have in Jesus' and 'Before the throne of God above' hit me with a sense of shame, worthlessness and fear. Some of the words of the songs seemed to be actually striking me. *Forfeit peace, pain, trials, discourage, weakness, despised and forsaken, depart, despair, guilt...* The words on the OHP screen took physical form and flung themselves at me, hitting me with all the force of their meanings, leaving me cowed in my pew. They were words of condemnation that caused me to feel that I had no place in church and I that should get out. I was arguing against this. It's not what the words mean. God does love me, and this 'me' does belong in church. It was hard to stand my ground.

I don't want to be subjected to this stuff. I don't know why it's become such a horrible feature of my mind at the moment. It's hard to trust God when I can only see an immediate threat rather than his long term (unrevealed) purpose.

Penny

Meanwhile, at home there is more than emotional dismantling going on around me. We've just had the wall taken down between the kitchen and dining room, making it open plan. It was a reasonable sized kitchen, but rather cut off from the living areas and so disconnecting me from family life while I made meals. Opening it up has brought an easy flow between rooms and given the whole area such light and space. What a difference one wall, or lack of it, can make!

March 17, 02:30
To: **John**
Subject: **the box again**

I'm confused. If it is God's will to unpack the box, why have I become vulnerable to such bad dreams and undermining thoughts and feelings? Why did I have such a bad experience in church if God is in charge of this? I thought pressing the 'send' button to say I would trust God with any unpacking he wanted to do would give me a safe way of doing that. The timing is nonsensical. There appears no reason for me to do this now and your impending sabbatical makes it worse. It would be an unreasonable extra load on your time right now, and the prospect of a false start is unsettling.

Yes, I was clear that God was asking me to do something about the box, but not specifically that it must be 'now'. He just asked for my willingness to trust him with it. Maybe it's been flagged up now so you can plan ahead for it on your return, before your diary gets filled in the autumn?

I don't want temporarily ruffled emotions to be driving this forward. I've not had any further word or picture about it since stating I would trust him. For these reasons, I'm half wanting to put this away. Perhaps I've got it wrong somehow. I don't want to negotiate with God. But then I'm not saying 'no', I'm just seeking calm clarity about what to do and when. I agreed not to pursue a 'why' as a condition of trusting him. If I'm bothered simply by stirred-up memories, that shouldn't mean there's any rush to deal with it in the spiritual sense; everything will still be in place to do that effectively later in the year.

So what might be a sensible and constructive 'interim' way forward? I affirm my commitment to trust God with unpacking the box once the timing is clearly right to both of us.

Penny

Well, it seems we might be going ahead. Despite all the problems of timing, we might be going ahead – and soon.

John and I have spoken about identifying a prayer partner for when we start prayer ministry. A few names were suggested, but did not seem right. Then I thought of Ruth, another minister in the town. I helped with doing an 'Easter stations' event in schools recently with John and Ruth. I just felt she was the right person for this, though I hardly know her. Perhaps her being in a different church, and one of John's good colleagues, is part of it. I sense there's something within her own nature and spirituality that speaks to me, that this is someone God is bringing forward for me to invite in. Bringing in another minister seems a rather outrageous drain on resources, to say the least. But when I mention her name to John he considers it readily enough. He will approach her.

I have started to experience difficulty with an area on the side of my stomach. I feel as though there is a physical lump within, which grows in direct proportion to this attention on the box. I find that eating enough to feel bulk within my stomach exacerbates the discomfort, and have begun to eject some meals to relieve this.

March 30, 21:41
To: **John**
Subject: **unpacking the box**

John,

Since the bad dreams have subsided, I have had something else manifest itself.

I'm not liking my body, my abdomen especially. I have an urge to pare it down (though not to be thin in itself). I have a constant hard lump in my stomach. I don't like eating, it's unpleasant and uncomfortable. I don't want it to be noticeable to others so I'm making myself eat little and often to counter it. This is so unusual for me. I know I've lost weight and I'm trying hard to ensure I don't drop below eight and a half stone but it's hard work to manage that.

The apprehension I have in keeping myself open to the prospect of unpacking the box is taking a lot of emotional energy and mental determination not to allow it to be any more detrimental to me. I understand the delays in dealing with it, but the waiting is really stressful.

Has Ruth been asked about being a prayer partner and, if so, what is the answer? Can we please address this soon in terms of asking God's direction so I then know whether I am to face things now, or be able to properly separate it for the time being? If I am able to shut it off, I can go back to normal.

Penny

3: Beginning

Journal entries and emails – April of Year 1

It's the first week of April. Ruth has agreed to support John in prayer ministry. I am relieved and daunted. We're going ahead.

I am at a public event this week that I know Ruth is attending. I find a moment to speak to her discreetly and briefly, to thank her for agreeing to help. I give her a small bunch of daffodils, telling her that I'm not sure if I will be able to show my gratitude to her later on, so ask her to accept these now as my expression of thanks for what she is doing. I want to cry for what she might later be caused to think of me, but I have to push that away and distance myself from it. The pressing need to move into the prayer ministry outweighs such a concern. At least – unlike John – she'll be easy to avoid in the future, after we have done this.

April 9, 03:03
To: **John**
Subject: **the box – rambling on**

John,

You said I could text if needed but that's not reasonable at this time of night and I just need to say some things and press 'send'.

I've actually had a blank on specific memories for the last couple of weeks; it's just the way I feel physically that's the issue. How much I feel it, fluctuates. But I feel gross inside, like a failed chrysalis that's distended and about to split, but there's only gunk to come out. I'm trying harder to make outward appearance counter that, to keep control... assuming it must be temporary and not what God wants, so trying not to get too concerned about it. And he gave me a most loving husband who sees me differently to my current self-image, and I know him to be a truthful man – so there's an oasis of hope.

It does seem hard work at the moment mentally and emotionally to keep a lid on all this. God is meant to go before us in things, but this feels like I'll be going in and then waiting to see if he joins me. Faith means I don't cancel the appointment.

I wanted to ask: where will we meet to pray? I'm concerned about privacy. But I'm sure you'll cover that.

Penny

This morning, as Daisie and I come out of the spinney, we turn left into the back field. The first part of this is a paddock area with two horses. 'Hello, horse,' I always say, if either amble over. I pull up a handful of the longer grass on my side of the fence and offer it on an open hand. I move on with Daisie, on with my conversation with God. Cutting through the copse on the left, I notice the contrast from the open field – thick rough grass is replaced by nettles and scrubby shrub branches. The tall trees impose a cool greyness on the ground. I am getting my heart ready.

This mid-April afternoon, I meet with John and Ruth for our first time, in the church vestry. The room is somewhat dilapidated, old wooden desks busy with stacks of papers, the floor swimming in piles of folders, boxes of communion wine and music stands. I feel wracked with trepidation, desperately wanting to run, yet determined to keep trusting God's leading. Turning back at this point might make it worse to return and face things later. I need to hold fast now. What's the matter with me? Why do I feel so very anxious?

We talk for a little while, John outlining why this meeting had come about and how we would approach this session: we will pray and wait on God for direction. John and Ruth will allow me to focus on my prayers, and they will pray out loud or read Bible verses as they feel appropriate, or else pray silently alongside me. It sounds so simple! It's actually so tough, a real struggle to hold my ground.

I start by trying to picture the attic, the scene of my four pictures. But I can't place myself there at all, as though there is resistance to it. John suggests I start at the bottom of the ladder where I had been standing, so I can then move up into the attic.

Quickly, I am confronted with a vivid image of being on that landing, with my foot on the bottom rung. But there is a dark oppressive presence at the foot of the staircase behind me, a presence that seems to threaten to come after me if I dare try to move up the ladder towards the attic above.

Previously, I had explained to John that 'entering the house' is something I need to do for myself, but that I also need to know that I have a safe connection to the outside. I likened it to the two of them standing outside, watching through the windows while I enter the rooms. I do not want them to see the detail in those rooms – the particular pieces of furniture and ornamentation – but simply to have sight of my figure within. They should be able to follow around to other windows as I move rooms, always keeping that connection with my position, though not looking at or becoming familiar with the contents of each room.

What I have not explained to either John or Ruth is that this attic is placed within a real house from my childhood, and now I am finding myself in something of a virtual-reality flashback within it – part memory and part visual representation of my experiences and their after-effects.

Impasse. I cannot move, and feel a great frustration and failure with how little has been accomplished. We decide I should withdraw from the house for now, so I come back 'outside'.

April 17, 16:21
To: **John; Ruth**
Subject: **box, attic and rooms**

John and Ruth,

I think I couldn't visualise the rooms of the house because it was too close for comfort, too close to the risk of seeing real rooms in my memories. Going back into those rooms was part of what happened in the police interviews, so trying to look straight into them yesterday was too direct, too fast, too scary a step. It's the events that happened in those rooms that are packed in the box. Going into those rooms could spring the lid of the box.

The footsteps on the stairs behind me were a shock – certainly from real life, but not a feature of the police interview time, so unexpected. Very threatening. I'm sorry that the shock remained more powerful than my assurance in God, and will pray more about that this week.

I couldn't bring myself to give any more detail before we started. But once we'd begun, I was fearful of being isolated if I did enter past scenarios. Maybe next time I should outline just a bit more of the 'who/where/what' about it all, so you know how to keep linked to me. I know I'm supposed to be trusting Jesus to be there with me, but I realise I need you two to bridge that for me to start. So I need you to have a better idea of where the other side – my side – of the bridge is.

Actually, remember my analogy of having you stand out on the drive while I went into the house? I said that the curtains would need to be opened, so you could see which room I was in and follow me around from outside? Yesterday it was more like trying to enter a boarded-up house.

I had a problem last night with body image after a big meal, this time with the urgency to purge. I slept badly, up from 3.30am, feeling physically gross.

I realise that the session was a point of no return. I can't go back on this process now. I so want the box cleared out. Staying on the landing is no good – it's not safe, it's a no-man's land. I told God I want my trust and assurance in him to be greater than the hold my fears have on me. He gave me calm. Now I need to walk in again and believe he'll be there too.

Penny

4: Helpless

Emails and journal entries – April of Year 1

April 21, 04:46
To: **John**
Subject: **box and rooms**

John,

I've been up a while – unsettled in my thoughts and uncomfortable with my body, experiencing the chrysalis image again. I only had soup last night, but still feeling not good. Not going with the urge though. Last week I had my fingers down my throat, but this time I stopped just before expelling, out of shame and wanting to defy it and not let that have charge. That was the big tension for the rest of the night, resisting until it was away from my stomach anyway. It's not really the food or how I look to others... it's how I feel I am from the inside coming out.

Please pray that I can manage this for the time being.

Penny

April 22, 03:32
To: **John**
Subject: **box and rooms**

John,

Am I mentally ill? I didn't think I was before. Feel like I'm being dismantled. But what if that's all that happens?

Penny

◈ ◈ ◈

April 22, 12:51
To: **John**
Subject: **box**

John,

I think God has been showing me this morning that disturbances are like storms, wherever they may manifest. When we are told how Jesus stilled a storm, he didn't change the water or the air, he changed the forces that were disturbing them. He has the authority and power to do that. Something is disturbed in me, but rather than look at the effects of it I should look for him to take charge of it. But it's hard while it's all raging.

I'm putting on such a front at the moment, sometimes feeling shaky inside, sometimes tearful. I'm extremely grateful for Michael's calm and steady love.

Penny

My confusion and sense of panic is rising, and I'm questioning the wisdom of this process. I have doubts pricking at me about John's level of knowledge and responsibility for what I have got into here. Yet I am completely helpless, unable either to control what is happening or to opt out of it. I have moments of despair and outrage at John for his culpability.

◈ ◈ ◈

April 26, 09:47
To: **John**

John,

I'm tired and low.

Last week I was upset with you. I'm sorry. I know it's not your fault how I feel at the moment. I knew the process of looking back at who I was would be uncomfortable, but I didn't realise how I'd lose my sense of self. It seems reckless and risky. I felt that you shouldn't have put me in the position you guided me into. I know it was my choice to say yes but I didn't know quite what would happen and maybe you did. I'm not sure if you knew what this would do to me or whether you left me partially ignorant in what I was agreeing to. I'm afraid of being left adrift and not resolving it all. There's more in the box than I realised.

Except sometimes when I'm with Michael, just the two of us, I'm struggling to maintain a fragile facade and afraid of people seeing through that. But that also makes me feel so false and horrid. Why don't I have good things out of this, not just the feeling of being pulled apart and lost?

Do you feel sure this is still the right thing? That I'll be okay? I don't have a sense of what good there'll be out of it, how I'll be okay with myself again. Please can you let me know what God is telling or showing you about it? Please can you pray that I can keep going?

Penny

Early May, and it's a day of pale sunshine as I walk into John's vestry, where he and Ruth are waiting for me. I always find the room reassuringly cluttered. Eclectically furnished. A corner computer desk hunkers up at the back, shouldering an untidy assortment of files. The low wooden table in the middle of the room serves as an overspill for more current resources, but it's inept and awkward as a coffee table. To my right, wedged between the door and the administrator's desk, is an old green armless sofa – the place where I sit alongside Ruth's calm and gentle presence and face my fears, confront my dismay.

I resolve to get through this session efficiently. Having got 'stuck' a couple of times now about the house, and wanting to be done with this process as quickly as possible, I begin now by briefly explaining a little more to John and Ruth about how the picture relates to a real place I lived in years ago. I outline my need to be sure that they will not pry or intrude without invitation about what I move among as I re-enter this house. I reiterate that I do not wish to describe the detail of my past, and they are not to try and offer comment or counsel on anything I relay to them. They concur.

We agree to proceed. John prays briefly, and I open myself to what God has for me.

The scene again unfolds around me. These pictures are not static or flat, more a vivid and three-dimensional scene; I can see and hear and feel what is here – was there – though I am choosing to walk it anew. I am at the foot of the ladder. I cannot proceed. I'm unable to enter the attic again, and I'm frustrated and perplexed by another impasse. This seems to go on for quite some time. I am rooted between the landing and the steps, and I wrestle to make sense of it or progress from it.

Previously, I have known when I had come to the end of what there was for me by seeing in my mind's eye a visual representation of 'pause'. I see this now, but rebel against it. Surely I cannot just pause at this point? I must press on, make some advance. I am determined to continue. Waiting seems ridiculous.

Then the picture shifts. I find myself in one of the bedrooms, the adults' room, and I feel a strong sense of intrusion and trepidation. I turn back after entering, and there is the tall chest of drawers behind the door. My guts lurch, and I am filled with disgust and dread. There before me on top of the chest is the makeshift grotesque shrine. Debasing and graphic literature is deliberately arranged, pages defiantly on show. Personal – very personal – items of mine are mounted centrally. More lurid publications are lined up along the floor in front. I remember it well.

His footstep. Panic rises within me. I must escape! I must not be caught before this display. But along with my urge to run is paralysis. Another footstep.

At this point the picture departs from what comes directly from memory, somehow depicting a spiritual dimension. Suddenly I am up near the ceiling, as though propelled away from a like-poled magnet. It is physically and mentally tough to resist. I will myself back to the floor, from where my feet could exit this trap. I find I can come down only a little way before being overwhelmed and pushed back up, though desperately fighting it. Back up into the top corner of the room, head pressed down by the ceiling, I am flooded with a sense of threat. Previously, it had been 'If you try to go up the steps, I'll get you!' Now it has become, 'If you keep trying, you will be cut off.'

The picture's gone. I find myself in deep emptiness, with a sense of bleakness and isolation. We pray, to safely close our time together. I am given some words of reassurance to hold onto – a promise from Isaiah that 'those who hope in the Lord will renew their strength. They will soar on wings like eagles; they will run and not grow weary, they will walk and not be faint.' And a verse from the Psalms, exhorting people facing fear and loneliness to keep their hope and confidence in God, and to 'wait for the Lord; be strong and take heart and *wait* for the Lord.'

5: Promise to tell

Journal entries and emails – May of Year 1

I've been awake since the early hours again, reading a book – *How to Trust God When Life Doesn't Make Sense* by Gary R Mayes – I found on my shelves. It's a book I've never actually looked at before. In it is a chapter on a king named Jehoshaphat, and the story of how he faces a crisis while continuing to trust God. The account, in the Old Testament book of 2 Chronicles, is essentially a 'how to' model for dealing with times of great threat, giving stages of response. I realise how this can be applied to so many testing situations and study it intensely, struggling to know how it can help me now.

Scanning between the book and my Bible, I learn that Jehoshaphat, faced with great impending national threat and having learned painful and costly lessons in the past, doesn't panic or react by emotional impulse. Instead he commits time and focus to prayer and fasting, to seeking God's will in the situation. His prayer is predominantly one of praise to God's power and faithfulness. Only when Jehoshaphat has spent time praising God does he briefly outline the problem at hand.

That seems significant to me. The proportions of praise and petitioning God are in their right balance, and it's all led by faith – not feeling. Jehoshaphat doesn't look at the mountain of the threat being faced, but on the God who can move such mountains. His prayer is honest and humble, putting his reliance completely in God. And then he and his whole nation wait… just wait… waiting in a situation that's painful, perhaps excruciating… waiting in trust, no matter what.

One thing that stands out to me is how Jehoshaphat doesn't allow feelings to dictate the course of events; he understands that faith can be a greater force. He chooses to focus on what he knows of the character of God, even in the face of great fear and uncertainty. Can I do that? Jehoshaphat did. While not dismissing real and understandable fears and doubts, he goes out to meet the foe, obeying what he feels to be God's guidance. With the worshipping musicians in front rather than the infantry, out they go. Not until the very last moment is it revealed that God has turned the two enemy factions against each other, and they've been completely decimated. The battle is over! God delivers them – without them having to engage in combat themselves.

I continue my study in the dawn light. Is this an example of God 'working for the good of those who love him' as St Paul wrote to the Romans? Not comfortable, not easy. Scary and costly.

Two key sentences from the story stay with me. 'For the battle is not yours, but God's,' Jehoshaphat is told. And, 'You will not have to fight this battle.' Yet the king's people *are* required to walk onto the battlefield before God brings about deliverance. And walking onto the battlefield is the prospect ahead of me.

May 7, 20:16
To: **John; Ruth**
Subject: **box**

Hi, John and Ruth,

The last thing God clearly said to me was 'just pause' but I allowed time pressures to influence my approach to yesterday's session. I decided that as God had given me clear insights and guidance the previous week that he would do that (and more?) again this week, and clear up the problems before us. I set the agenda for him – instead of truly waiting on God.

I do not know quite what God is doing with me, or what the outcome or purpose is. But I do know that God loves me, is with me, and I trust him. I will wait in dependence on him. Whatever the process entails, I actually have a sense of quiet confidence and anticipation of seeing his purposes revealed and glory shine through it all.

I can see that what happened last time we met was a kind of banging of the lid of the box to try to scare me away. So this is a pause to acknowledge the fears and yet still be ready to walk on in faith.

Today I will wait, I will praise, I will trust.

Penny

The sunlight washes the field in front of me as I step over the stile between the thin copse and the neighbouring paddock. Daisie scoots over ahead and is on the alert for where the horses might be, and detecting whether their owner's two large dogs might hurtle over and re-establish their friendly dominance of the territory. But the field's empty, and we meander over the rough tussocks towards the stile opposite.

I hear the voice clearly: 'Will you tell the story?'

I am astonished. I stand in the quiet, the words reverberating in my soul. Daisie's lead gently tugs me forward, and I walk on in contemplation.

I am appalled by what I have been asked. There is no sense of progress in the sessions at all. We haven't got anywhere! I do not quite understand the purpose of it all for myself, let alone for anyone else, and consider it a deeply private process. Even if matters were resolved, I would not want my experiences 'told'. I tell God that what he is suggesting is ludicrous.

It's two days later, as I cross the paddock, and the routine is again interrupted by the unexpected question, this time with a preface: 'This story should be told. Will you tell the story?'

I do not have an answer. What comes to mind are all the times when I would pray the prayer of Jabez from the Bible: *'Oh, that you would bless me indeed and enlarge my territory! Let your hand be with me, and keep me from harm so that I will be free from pain.'*

Defensively, I exclaim that this isn't what I'd meant in my petitions. This extraordinary anecdote of one man's request to God and its simple granting, told in the book of Chronicles, has been called 'an exquisite gem among a mountain of earthy genealogy'.

I tell God that while I realise I've been praying that prayer for about 11 years now (keeping a small card with it printed on in my purse and often on my kitchen wall) and I know too that I've been asking to serve more and have my 'territory' enlarged, this is not how I imagined that happening. Not this – anything but this! What would be the good purpose in it?

A few days later, I hear the words again, accompanied by an intriguing condition. 'Will you tell the story? When you have moved forward, will you tell the story?'

Moved forward... *When* I have moved forward... There is condition and promise in this phrasing. It suggests that God is going to take me to a different place from the bleak and confusing one I inhabit now. I cannot envisage what that place might be, but I can trust enough – just – that I will be moved forward. I am not required to tell the story until that has happened, until it is a right time with God. There is reassurance.

In spite of my qualms, I say yes.

6: Another name

Journal entries – May of Year 1

It's late morning as I cross the road to the church. Cars enter and exit the adjoining High Street one-way system. People on foot make their way to the corner supermarket or to the small pedestrian shopping precinct leading through to the main shopping area. I navigate the traffic, heading for the entrance to the church coffee shop. Familiar faces acknowledge me as I walk in, stepping around the wooden tables, giving berth to shopping bags slumped against chair legs. Nodding, I hope my eyes show some of my heart's appreciation for these friends, even while my set mouth betrays my inner unsettledness.

I'm finding personal contact with people increasingly hard to cope with. I don't want people to see my vulnerability. At times, it's as though contact tears little strips of my being off the bone. I am relieved to reach the far door which takes me away from the humming chatter and into the corridor leading to the vestry.

Pushing open the door, I find John and Ruth standing together. Their words trail away. I am welcomed, and spend a few minutes in small talk with Ruth while John fetches mugs of coffee.

We review how things have been since we last met. The last scheduled meeting had been abandoned when I'd arrived in shock after receiving the news of a friend's tragic death. It was not the time to engage further with the process. I speak for a little while about those circumstances and the emotional fallout generated, and then assure them I am ready to focus on the business in hand.

Ruth asks me how I feel things stand for me at this point. I realise how much I have come to trust both Ruth and John – Ruth for her warmth and gentle savviness, John for his dynamism, and both of them expressing their deep commitment to wanting to see people grow in lives of faith. We are all aware of the impending time of John's sabbatical, when their direct support will necessarily be withdrawn. I tell them I'm okay, holding steady if a little dazed. I had felt dismayed in recent weeks that all would not be concluded before the summer break, that we seemed just to be uncovering more and more mess instead of reaching a neat resolution. But somehow I sense this is part of the plan, a blueprint from which I cannot construct solid shape but which I trust has intention and security built into it. One thing we consistently agree on at each session is that this is all in God's timing and control.

I tell them what I have heard during my morning walks. I have a knot in my stomach as I do so, aware that the possibility now has witnesses. My accountability to John and Ruth is not a problem in itself, for I know they will respect my responses. But speaking out the idea embeds the reality of making my story public – and makes it even more daunting.

Ruth asks me if I have any sense of *how* the telling of the story is meant to be. Will I write it? No. I tell them I'm meant to speak it, I think. That feels a disquieting admission! Public speaking is not something I'm comfortable with or practised in. To lay open such personal matters…

And what 'story' anyway? What is this all about? Or leading to? I hold onto the phrase '*when* you have moved forward' as I explain a picture I've seen, of telling my story here, in the church.

We pray, particularly asking for protection over me. Our time together is calm. Ruth reads a Bible passage that refers to individuals being called by name by God. She uses my name: Penny. It prompts an unexpected reaction.

'That's not my name,' I blurt out.

Silence. Even I am surprised by my words.

I say again, 'That's not my name. Penny is not my proper name.'

'What do you mean? What is your proper name?'

'Peppy. My name was Peppy. That's my proper name – and I want my name back.'

This is something that's been privately brewing in my heart for a little while, but suddenly it bubbles up, the hot softness of my words sliding over my heart like a balm. I realise the urgency and deep significance of this within me.

I was Peppy as a child, Peppy to my dad up to the time my parents divorced and he left. I was always Peppy at primary school. I changed it to Penny to avoid standing out after some mild playground teasing and in tandem with the changed family dynamic that fractured my sense of security and identity. In sporadic contact with my dad over the years, and his eventual return to closer living and relationship to me in my mid-twenties, I was always Peppy to him, spoken with great warmth and fondness. And a shortened form is used by a few family members still. With my dad's death a few years ago, and less contact with those relatives, I feel that my real name is being lost.

Now I find I yearn to reclaim it. I have thought about the meanings of the two names. Penny (from Penelope) means 'weaver of threads' from a story in Homer's *Odyssey*. Discovering this gives me a wry smile. I feel I am trying to make sense of the underside of a complicated piece of weaving, with rather too many loose ends. One meaning of Peppy, I have discovered, means 'God will enlarge'. Given my longstanding prayer echoing the words of Jabez, this impacts me deeply.

'So what do you think is the significance of all this?' Ruth asks.

'I think that God knows and wants that part, the Peppy part, of who I am brought out and enlarged, as well as the Penny I have become since then,' I say.

Michael has begun calling me Peppy in private. I reflect on our love and how it's such a vital part of why I am able to go forward within all this turmoil. His craggy face reminds me of his rock-solid character, which is accompanied by true gentleness of nature. He knows what's important in life and that accounts for his lovably scruffy appearance and quiet resistance to convention. When he plays the piano or fiddle, usually extempore, he spills lilting splashes around the melodies, making the music flow and sparkle.

So now I am Peppy to him. And John and Ruth say they will try to use it. It feels right, though I accept this is something just between us. Changing my name at my age could be awkward for those too long familiar with calling me Penny. Its healing use will be contained within a small circle, and in gratitude I savour every utterance of it. Our time together in prayer is infused with reassurance. I bathe my soul in the promises God gives us through his Word, the Bible, and feel at peace.

The afternoon church group – mainly elderly and most with some disability or illness – that I lead in Bible study, have felt particularly trying today. Normally I cherish this group. I feel humbled by them. They have shown me so many glimpses of God in the unexpected. But today my mind struggles to follow the non sequiturs thrown up, and I am silently testy. We are supposed to be looking at the passage in Ephesians about 'the armour of God' which protects us against enemy action. Ordinarily I would find this edifying, helpful. Today I sullenly reflect that maybe Paul should have mentioned 'girding with grace' and putting on 'a sense-of-humour protector'.

7: Waiting

Journal entries – June to August of Year 1

It's late June now and I'm feeling unsettled. I happen to hear something on the radio about the impact of abuse in a family. The question of other people's knowledge of what happened during my childhood and their response to that is upsetting me. There were people who knew what I was subjected to – including, I suspect, my mother – yet they turned a blind eye to it. This suggests to me that I wasn't worth protecting, that I was of no value to anyone.

Yet these same people are as loved and precious to God as I am, possibly in need of healing themselves. They must be forgiven. I struggle with that.

July, and I'm reading *Forgive and Forget* by Lewis B Smedes. God is gently but persistently showing me that I need to forgive. I have become calm, matter-of-fact and accepting about this. I recognise that I hold what the book refers to as 'passive hatred' – not anger, not malice, but something justified as self-protection – and it's an ugliness within me which must be healed. I will walk that path of forgiving.

I have begun to share with one or two Christian friends what I am going through, why I am having prayer counselling, how I need to forgive. Voicing this, having it 'witnessed' by others, guards me against denying it or keeping it hidden. It makes me accountable.

It's not all plain sailing. Some days I feel lost, bewildered and in pain. I struggle specifically when I feel God is asking me to get in touch with someone from my past who has hurt me. I hold on to a couple of verses from Isaiah 42: 'He will not break the bruised reed, nor quench the dimly burning flame. He will encourage the fainthearted, those tempted to despair. He will see full justice given to those who have been wronged.' I read *The Inner Voice of Love* by Henri Nouwen, which strikes so many chords.

In mid-August we spend a week as a family in a holiday cottage, going out each day to explore local beaches, wander streets from bygone days and toast marshmallows over a mountainside campfire.

Towards the end of our time away, Michael, George and I go to see some beautiful waterfalls. Sheep roam freely nearby, unfortunately so freely that we even see the rotted remains of one caught on a small island in the stream. Then we realise that a sheep has got stuck in a faster flowing section, possibly after jumping over a steep bank and being unable to negotiate its way back. Michael sets off to investigate, while George and I head for the cafe at the bottom of the hill. Just as we are getting concerned over how long he's been gone, a lone figure is seen coming out of the trees, looking shaky and bedraggled. One trouser leg is rolled up over the knee, blood trickling down to the ankle. Michael!

He relates the story over coffee and cake. When he found the sheep, it was trapped on a ledge in a gorge, at the foot of a deep waterfall. He waded upstream to reach it, knowing that at any moment it might plunge in any direction. It was safe on the ledge where it stood, but couldn't go anywhere without being in deep water. So Michael edged closer from a slightly elevated position, realising that he would have to wade through the water and then make a lunge for it. He was unsure how the sheep might react. But in the event, he was surprised to find the sheep quite complicit, almost as though it knew he was there to rescue it. So he had the sheep firmly in his grasp. Then the thought occurred, 'Now what do I do?'

There was only one way to go, of course – back downstream some distance to where the bank was relatively low. Then he became aware that on the path about 15 feet above, many camera-clicking tourists were finding him the focus of attention. The mission had to succeed now! He progressed slowly downstream, hauling the sheep over slippery rocks in the cold flow of water, simply hoping to make it to where the slope was low enough to release the sheep. The slope was steep, dense with creeping ivy and thick brambles, and before long Michael was trembling with exertion. At one point he had to lower himself backwards down a section of rock, squeezing through a narrow gap between two trees. Taking the full weight of the sheep, he committed one leg to take the drop, then realised that his trailing leg was firmly caught with bramble, preventing him from moving. He couldn't go back up because of the weight of the sheep, and he couldn't hack at the bramble without letting go of the sheep and failing in his venture. The only option was to forcibly pull with the ensnared leg to break the bramble. This took an agonising couple of minutes. As layers of skin gave way before vicious thorns, the sheep was totally relaxed and trusting in his arms, calmly nibbling moss and lichen from the rocks beside them. The bramble, as thick as Michael's thumb, finally yielded. After about 15 tortuous minutes, they were safe. He lifted the sheep up over the last four feet to a rough bank where it quickly made a bid for freedom, ignoring the spontaneous applause from the gathered onlookers. Michael made his way to the shop and cafe about 400 yards below, happily receiving a souvenir toy sheep as a memento of his heroic rescue mission.

We go to the village church on the last day, and I feel prompted to go forward for prayer at the end of service. There's some delay, some confusion in finding someone to leave the coffee queue and come over to me, as I sit waiting quietly in a side pew. I am put off by this, wishing I hadn't bothered. A middle-aged woman finally hurries over and I try to usher away my irritation. I tell her just that I am 'in the process of healing'. She accepts this without further inquiry, and prays alongside me. While I silently pray and reflect on my childhood days, I say several times, 'I forgive them, I forgive what was done, I forgive...' It's an act of sheer will rather than anything heartfelt. The woman then says she felt God saying, 'Out of brokenness will come wholeness.' I am moved to quiet tears. Finding Michael, we walk back to the cottage, holding close to each other and to the promise given.

Who I am to Michael – my sheep rescuer – has been unchanged through all this. He loves me for who I was when we met and who I have been since. He loves me for who I am. He always knew I had a 'past', never wanted to know the detail, accepting me for who he knows me to be in the here and now.

Who I am to God, that other sheep rescuer, is unchanged. Not just from when I changed to accept him. Who I am to him has always been complete and constant. I am only affected by what I perceive of myself. I am and continue to be made new. This is greater than the wrongs of the past… a work in progress. God fully knows me, yet still to him I am precious, loved and worth his care and attention. How awesome is that?

8: The inner and the outer

Journal entries – August to September of Year 1

During the summer months while John is away, I am having gentler ongoing conversations with God rather than the more dramatic experiences.

For the time being I can allow the lid of the box to remain closed but unlocked. The rooms in my memories are not to be emptied. I just need the things within them not to overpower and shackle me any longer – cleared of destructive power rather than cleared out – and for me to be able to move in it and through it. The box is left unlocked and accessible.

Waiting. John, remembering both the origin of the name Penny and my current situation, left me with the words of a poem called *The Divine Weaver.* This talks of the weaving of the colours of our lives, of how the dark threads are woven along with the gold and silver ones. I am reassured. What appears messy from the underside has form, intent, beauty and pattern on the other.

During this time I am also reading Henri Nouwen's book *The Wounded Healer*, and finding it so helpful. And I make what I call 'Ebenezer boards'. This term Ebenezer comes from the book of 1 Samuel in the Bible, where a 'stone of help' was erected as a tangible monument to remind the people of how God had acted for them in the past and could be trusted with whatever was ahead.

My particular 'Ebenezer stones' are two picture frames, each with three apertures. In one I have a picture like my box in the attic – open as a symbol of my forward-looking hope. My name, Peppy, is printed across one window. In another is mounted a small card with the prayer of Jabez (about 'enlarging my territory') printed on it. Two more display a poem by Connie Faust, called *Walkin' in the Valley of Berracah* which describes Jehoshaphat's act of faith and God's answer to prayer that he and his people receive in that valley of blessing and praise. Finally, there is a representation of one way that I see the word 'pause', a reminder that waiting can sometimes be an active way of obeying God's will. My 'Ebenezer boards' give me reassurance and strength. I carry them from room to room with me, to keep them constantly in view.

While all the emotional undercurrent swirls around in my inner life, my outer life continues, full of extraordinary ordinariness.

There is a sad death involving our next door neighbours, both in their early nineties: she, a delightful and feisty soul, though isolated by deafness; he a marvellous gentleman, knowledgeable and considered in his ways. Not long ago they were stunned to be told that she was terminally ill, though nothing had been apparent before the blood test results. They faced the dismay of realising that age limited what treatment was offered; that in fact an end was inevitable soon, no matter what was or wasn't done for her. And then she began to decline.

A hospital bed was set up in their dining room, affording her a view through the French windows across their beautifully tended garden and over the undulating fields beyond. We were privileged to be warmly welcomed each time we visited, sharing in the precious last days of a couple who had lived and loved together for nearly 70 years. Each day as I walked Daisie, I paused at the wrought iron fence at the bottom of their garden and waved to her. Her arm raised more feebly in return as the days progressed.

She died quietly one day, moments after her husband had spoken gentle reassurance to her as he went to fetch her a drink.

We spend an evening with him. He speaks of loss and sadness, of all her admirable qualities and the memories they shared. He is starting to look into the aching chasm her death has brought. Nothing can ease the grief that he no longer has this wife he calls 'simply the best'. Such bereavement can only be acknowledged and we want to be beside him as he bears its sad weight. They were not churchgoers but the funeral is held at our village church. I pray that some comfort will reach into the bleak recesses and sustain him for the time ahead.

August has given way to September. Today a sparrow fell down the chimney, so Michael and I get very sooty reaching up through the stove pipe to grab it while it flutters manically. A quick wash under the kitchen tap and it's soon back in the hawthorn hedge with the rest of the chirruping colony. Meanwhile, the hen chicks that hatched a few weeks ago are out of their protective wire run, roaming free and jostling for grain, pellet feed and bread with the bustling 'big girls'.

Since term started, it's been a busy time with the puppet team that I lead, but this week there is a break. Just as well, really. I get a text from George asking me if he can bring one of his mates back from town. I discover that this time there are, in fact, five of them and, yes, they'd like lunch, they're starving! Oh, and one of them is a vegetarian. What to serve? While they take twenty minutes to enjoy the rope swing in the nearby wood, I have a quick rummage. I produce a party platter of Indian snacks from the bottom of the freezer. (Where did that come from? Forgotten from Christmastime, perhaps?) There's also some garlic bread and two bowls of pasta – one with cheese sauce and one with pesto. They wash it down with ginger beer and fruit juice. The 'rock-gods' tell me I'm awesome, and I'm happy to take the accolade. I always welcome George's friends but – to be honest – I am looking forward to the passing of the 'metal' phase which, hour upon hour and day after day, tests my nerves. Their music may be 'heavier' than my tastes but thankfully the accompanying lifestyle doesn't seem too wild just yet.

Elly is spending two weeks away in France with a family we are friends with. She needs to improve her French for her GCSE, and this is such a lovely opportunity. Within days there is a problem in communication – technologically speaking – as she has dropped the sim card out of her mobile phone and can't find it. She's anxious about being so out of touch. However she can access the internet sometimes, so I send a few tongue-in-cheek emails to reassure her.

Ah, ma chère Elly-la-Nora,

Pourquoi tu n'es pas cherche le sim ? Ca c'est très mauvais. Le tut tut.

Aujourd'hui Daisie est dans the chien-maison parce ce qu'elle s'enfuir de l'autre cote de la rue. Les poussins est en peu scraggly mais très adorable, bien sur.

George aller au ville avec son amis, dépenser tout son argent (beaucoup de bonbons)... merde! Il n'a pas du prix du billet en train. Papa aller au ville dans la voiture... et il se dire, 'bien paradis!'

Quel temps fait-il? Surtout il fait du soleil, mais deux fois il pleut à torrents. Très bien pour le jardin, eh?!

Cherche le blinking sim!

Je t'adore, ma fille, elle ma manque!

Maman xx

9: Falling flesh

Journal entries and emails –
September to October of Year 1

I am struggling more acutely with social contact. I avoid people where possible. Added to that, there is the ongoing stress of difficulty with retaining food, accompanied by my escalating loathing of my own torso. I feel part of my side is grotesquely distended from within – even though I acknowledge it's not necessarily physically visible. This constantly gnaws at my self-image and inhibits my ability to eat normally. I routinely excuse myself from the family meal table. My family comment but, as they know I am trying hard to take in small nutritious snacks, they are not pressing me to face larger meals.

John returned from sabbatical at the start of the month, but we haven't been able to meet. He is, of course, swamped by the backlog of work demanding attention.

I find myself feeling sudden peaks of spikiness towards John whenever I am in his presence. It's disconcerting, as it seems totally unreasonable. Puzzlingly, he does not seem to realise the strength of feeling surging up in me. I am trying to work out what's going on.

September 30, 20:51
To: **John**
Subject: **irritation**

John,

I realised something after speaking to you today. You heard my outward voice, but I heard my inner voice. I *was* spiky inside because I felt rattled by your presence, because I'm reminded of what I need you to walk me through again. Your return from sabbatical is welcome, but has an unsettling aspect because it coincides with a new need to go back into dark rooms – needed, yet dreaded too. I know you'll say an apology isn't really required. And I do understand about being patient while you get everything else sorted out.

Peppy

Early October and today we resume prayer ministry.

Ruth's not had time for breakfast so brings a plate of toast through from the church coffee shop. Not for the first time recently, the smell makes me reel. It's obnoxious, repellent, and I have to ask her to remove it. Ruth gently exclaims at how tiny I appear. I am seven and a half stone, battling to maintain this borderline level, fearful of it being noticeable through all my layers of clothing. I despise the sight of my nakedness, and have been dressing and undressing away from Michael's eyes for some time.

I am aware of the catching and clawing of fabric against my side as we talk, and sit as still as I can to minimise the distraction. I don't want any attention to be given to what I have been driven to do in coping with the unleashing of my hidden emotional pain.

When John leaves the room briefly, Ruth quietly asks me if I am eating properly. I feel that the rug has been pulled from under me. This is the only thing I feel I have any bit of control over. Everything else is spinning wildly out of control. Somewhere within the vortex, a fragment of me knows that God must be in charge, yet my situation feels deeply frightening, confusing, getting worse by the day.

I protest that I am fine, that it's under control. She carefully enquires if there's anything else I might want to tell her. I am cornered, knowing I must say that I have done something to myself, to my body. Having spoken its ugliness, I know I must show it too.

Its power needs to be stripped away.

For the last few weeks I have been self-harming, driven to try to obliterate my side. It's what it represents to me that I can't abide. It's the place where his hand would first make contact under the covers, in which instant I would find myself paralysed by fear and intimidation… frozen, horrified and disgusted by my inability to move away, by my complicity in what then took place.

John returns to the room. I ask him to turn away as I lift my clothing and stand in shame, allowing Ruth to look at my burned side. Repeated attempts to remove this traitorous flesh have left me with wounds in various stages of rawness and scabbing. I have not dressed the wounds. I have been perversely welcoming of the way fabric tugs and grates over them, hoping the flesh will all eventually fall away. Some areas have begun to seep a pale thick fluid, and I have hoped the rot would go deep.

I adjust my clothing and sit down silently for a few moments. It's in the light now, which will make it harder to continue. In dark mood, I ask if we can turn our attention to our prayers.

The picture quickly opens around me. I'm at the bottom of the stairs. The bottom! I am so dismayed. This is not where I need to be – I need to be at the top, and ascending the ladder into the attic, surely. Together, we haul through a long frustrating time of seeking understanding about being downstairs, and the failure to move at all up the stairs. At the top of the stairs is the dark presence, waiting just around the corner of the landing. There too lies the old sense of threat. I need to get up those stairs, but I am unable to take even one step.

Eventually I see the representation of 'pause' that presents itself in my mind's eye each time the purpose of that day's ministry has been exhausted, and disconsolately I accept the signal. We ask for God's work to continue in me, for him to be in charge of however this unfolds. I have learned the lesson to wait when I should.

10: On the banana skin

Emails and journal entries – October of Year 1

October 14, 20:33
To: **John; Ruth**
Subject: **box**

You've asked me a couple of times how long I think this is going to take. What I am reluctant to ask back is, 'How long do *you* think?' Maybe I should hear your answers, because the way I've tried to keep framing things has tripped me up.

Ruth, I've made my bracelet. Thank you for suggesting it. I have used a red glass heart and a clear glass cross for it – and it does help to have that tangible reminder of God's love in view on my arm. I think I sometimes don't receive what you're saying very well in the moment, I'm not sure why. Maybe sometimes your kindness throws me. Or maybe sometimes it's the fact that you're so at ease in your own skin, with who you are. But actually your kindness is taken in, and appreciated, even if later and on my own.

Having had things I felt sure I wanted to address today, I seemed to just become lost in it all and I don't know what we achieved today, spiritually. I know you challenged me, but what was God saying? I'm not supposed to be getting counselling from you, I'm supposed to be unpacking before God. I find it most difficult when I don't know what he's saying.

I've been willing to face the box, and let him use what's in it if need be. Why is the unrelenting dismantling of me necessary?

October 15, 09:09
To: **John; Ruth**
Subject: **box**

Hi,

It seems to me that what I do with my eating is surely just a way of coping with the difficulties I'm associating with it. It's an interim measure and I'm being careful that overall I do take in what I need, regardless of how I feel about it, so that how things are in my mind doesn't have complete charge. What I'm trying very hard to 'give way' in is with the spiritual side of things, which is the most important. What would happen if I gave way on a practical level with food? Either I'd eat less to ease that stress, or take advice to eat more and agitate the emotional load more. Either way doesn't seem to be a helpful one. I'm bothered about having the focus shift onto side effects rather than cause. If you're in a runaway carriage with a team of wild horses, you'd hang on tight to any rein you could grab, even if it took a while for order to return on the journey.

Peppy

October 15, 15:16
To: **John; Ruth**
Subject: **box**

I've checked my bmi and it is still just in the okay range. I'll make sure it stays that way.

I didn't want to 'go up the stairs' because of who was standing at the top. I can't even approach the attic, and having an unlocked lid on the box means stuff is not properly contained. This has been hard.

After two days of inner ranting, I woke this morning with a sense of 'ease off, stop trying so hard'... like a person drowning who thrashes around to the point of fighting their rescuer. If they truly trusted and relaxed, they could so much more easily be brought to a safe place. Well, that sounds reasonable and easy, then...

Peppy

I have started an evening class, a foundation course in Christian faith and service. The course was recommended to me by John earlier in the summer. It seems the right way forward, yet sitting among 14 conformists who all appear quite stable, I quickly become doubtful of my place.

We'd been asked to bring an item with us this week to represent something of our faith journey. In desperation to come up with anything, I look through a neglected stash of cards and notes kept in the large pocket of my old Bible. I unfold a slip of lined paper, a handwritten note. It had been given to me 13 years before, the year after I became a Christian and then found myself thrown into unwelcome single parenthood and depression. The words, the echo from the past, floored me: 'Penny, you have started well. God is laying a call upon you. Some people are given small things to be faithful in, and some are given greater things. You will be given a greater task, not because you are great, but because you will obey.'

I also come across a greetings card from years ago. There's a cartoon picture of a penguin who has slipped on a banana skin in the middle of a wide expanse of ice. Inside a friend, encouraging me during those hard years of sole and stumbling responsibility for my young children, had written, 'For all those times when the banana skin is just waiting, remember *what is impossible with man is possible with God* (Luke 18:27).'

I hurriedly decide that the card will do. I could make light of things with it. The slip of paper is inside it, as I want to ponder it further, and so I take them both in my folder.

During the evening we take turns to share what we have brought. When it gets to my turn, I describe the card but go on to explain how it's not an icy landscape I inhabit now, it's a desert – and I don't want to be here. My despair suddenly spills out. I am shaken by what I am revealing before so many almost-strangers. I even read the note from the piece of paper, and find more words tumbling out of my mouth – that I know God's call on me requires me to face the hidden corners of my past and to be alongside others who also fear lids springing open on them. I am to tell my story, and place myself in public in doing so. But in truth I don't want it. I don't want this call. I am devastated to hear my own admission. I'm afraid and don't want to go where God is leading me.

Oh, why did I say all that?

A silence hangs heavy in the room for a few moments before the tutor thanks me and moves on to the next person. I feel as though I've let off a depth charge and the stunned impact on the room only slowly subsides. It's not going to be easy returning to the class.

11: Stuck in the muck

Journal entries and emails – October of Year 1

My friend Dani and I have a school assembly with our puppets first thing.

Dani's a visual thinker like me, unfussy, grounded and straightforward, and someone who has really encouraged me in being creative. We are easy together and have fun, especially working with our puppets.

Today, the last-minute cutting out of a final prop results in me gashing my finger with the craft knife. I discover I've no plasters in the bathroom cabinet. Then Elly announces I have to get her to the station earlier than expected. So, clutching wads of tissues in my hand, I drop her off and go to Dani's, interrupting their family breakfast with a practical opportunity for her husband's first-aid training.

The presentation at the assembly is something of a departure. We do a role reversal, with John arriving late, disorganised and cheeky, and Billy the puppet being exasperated by this. John then pretends to get very cross at Billy for being hypocritical, at which Billy gets the huff and 'walks out'. Silence in the school hall. This isn't what they were expecting. After talking about falling out and forgiving – and with Billy doing a rap poem on the conversation between Jesus and Peter about how many times we should forgive – Billy says sorry, John says sorry, they forgive each other and make up. There are some relieved oohs and aahs from around the hall.

Forgiveness, like so much of faith, is a tightrope. On one of my windows at home I have a painting on glass, made by my friend

Vera, who had seen the scene she created twice in dreams. Green and yellow hues glow in the streaming sunshine. The picture shows feet balanced on a rope suspended high above the countryside. The words alongside the picture express the fact of faith being as wobbly as a tightrope and emphasise the need to press on, not looking down, not looking to hide.

I reflect on the times I've felt wobbly, on the freezing-in-fear moments and let-me-off-now days. I also consider how the steps occasionally seem easier, the relief and satisfaction of courage allowing toes to inch ahead and soles to rebalance. For me, for now, the rope has stopped swaying so unnervingly. The balancing pole is steady. I can focus on the next step, even if I do wobble again. I imagine a bearded bloke is on the rope just behind me, reminding me, 'Relax, we've got you!'

Today, Sunday, has been one of those days of balancing the family tightrope. It's the sort of day when all sorts of spats and exasperations are going on within the family, yet you're somehow all close and secure too.

At the moment, Sundays are not always restful. We are temporarily using our upstairs church halls while some refurbishment is carried out in the sanctuary. This means a lot of hands-on help is needed, setting out and packing away chairs and other furniture each week before the service. Michael had signed us up to do this task this morning, but over breakfast I agitate about our lateness in getting ready. Once at church, he's slow over the task – possibly a passive resistance to my agitation. The general edginess continues through the morning. Elly is periodically snappy and venting it on Michael and George, much to their bewilderment. I quietly ask if she might be feeling a little hormonally challenged – at which she wails forlornly and both men jump up, shouting, 'Yes! A lot!'

Back home afterwards, Elly and George say they will cook lunch. The preparation goes on for ages. Michael and I bow out for a while to drop in at a friend's birthday 'do', though I am quickly frayed by the social interaction, so we return home. Another hour is spent diplomatically guiding a rescue of the meal while not 'interfering'. In the end it's lovely; we disregard the late hour, sit down together and commune. Soul food, indeed.

As the family dinner finishes, a light banter continues to be enjoyed as we relax back in our chairs. I have been quietly to-ing and fro-ing, fetching and clearing – normal for me but also at times a screen, holding me back from eating. George is tossing quirky asides to Michael about some anecdote I've lost track of.

'What could it *be*... or a *wasp*?' says Michael with feigned incredulity.

The chuckling is gliding over the table, warming the room. I return from the utility room and hear them making up silly phrases: 'Tender Brenda with the slender, er...'

'Kneecaps!' calls George.

Elly tells them they're ridiculous, but her smile gives away her affection. The chatter and laughter spread between us and I revel in it.

Elly is so much made in my image but, as a relative once remarked, without the broken spirit. Socially at ease, she really enjoys being with people and I love her effusive and outgoing personality, despite the adolescent tendency to want to dominate. George is also warm and loyal, though introverted and seemingly distracted, deeply thoughtful and compassionate. He is most content at home and with just a small circle of people and is happiest when absorbed in creating music.

I love my family.

Another Sunday. It's an all-age family service. Michael sits with me in one of the side rows, partially blocking me from the rest of the congregation. I find it difficult to look to the front where John is leading. Each time I see him, such anger wells up in me. In the last few weeks I have had to make conscious decisions to avert my eyes because of this reaction, and to hold myself at a distance from him physically. The flash images in my mind develop; I repeatedly see myself grab him by the lapels and pin him up against the wall.

Recently, on occasions when I've needed a brief word with John about something, I've had to stay on the threshold of the vestry, keeping a hand on the door as a restraint to these urges. My anger is getting harder to contain, even while I know it's totally unreasonable.

During the children's talk, John uses an illustrated story of a duck whose truck gets stuck in some muck, and who is helped out by a frog, a sheep and a goat. Instead of hearing a story of loving sacrifice, I hear a story of sneering personal mockery, of someone who is just stuck in the muck where they belong. Utter rage begins to swirl in me, along with despair.

Following the service, over coffee, I'm desperate to go home but have to stay alongside Michael, who needs a few minutes to speak to someone. I follow mutely, willing everyone to stay away from me.

John approaches. A vivid picture plays on a loop in my mind. With John pinned against the wall, I am furiously smashing his head back against it. Every fibre of my being strains. My hands want to play this out. I am teetering, appallingly uncertain of what is image and what could quickly become real action.

I manage to place myself behind Michael, who is chatting amiably with someone. I stare hard at the floor, tugging on Michael's arm to signal my need to leave. Thankfully he realises I have reached some kind of limit. I hold firmly to him as we turn and walk out of the room.

I'm in the midst of a maelstrom. Dark echoes of a past rage lash my mind like battering wind and stinging rain, whipping from every side. This isn't about John. I cannot see anything beyond what beats against me. I *am* rightly to be despised. I'm exposed for the despicable wretch that I am. I am unmasked. I stay at home, withdrawn, lost in my tumult. I take myself to the spare bedroom and consider what is bubbling up and spitting scalding splashes into my mind, what begins to boil over and overflow through my laptop.

October 17, 12:58
To: **John**
Subject: **box**

Stuck in the muck or mud? That doesn't begin to describe where I am. I feel like I've been standing in a pile of shit for a long time, holding up a rose stem and asking people if it looks nice, if they like its fragrance. *Don't look down, look at the bloody rose.* Now the rose is rapidly wilting, and I've slipped over. As if that wasn't bad enough, I'm being asked from somewhere what the shit smells like. I can't keep holding my breath.

I know what fear smells like. I know what the stench of shame is. I don't want to be flooded with it again and again. I think my face is about to be pushed right into it all. The question is not so much 'what does it smell like from up here?' as 'what is it like when it's right there, physically filling your nostrils, when you're right down there and in it?' I hate it, but the more I struggle the shittier I get. And I can't remember what the rose was like any more.

Penny

12: The gardener

Journal entries and emails – late October to November of Year 1

A couple of days later, and the storm has abated. Peace, blessed peace! I've had a picture, a most wonderful picture.

I stand by my back doorstep, looking out over the garden and the fields beyond. Beside me, to my left, half turned towards me, is Jesus. He's dressed in old gardening clothes, clearly grubby and perspiring slightly from the work. He wears a battered floppy-brimmed hat, and is at ease with me as we stand together. Nothing is spoken and everything is said within the loving companionship. He knows me, and knows all that has needed to be dug through.

In the corner of the garden is the compost heap. I know it is what we have been turning over. It will be what we later work into various patches and borders around the land.

I notice something. There is a particular stain on his clothes. Old blood and fluid has seeped through and shows that place of wounding on him. It is not hidden, remaining always a part of his being.

He has been with me all along and he understands me with the deepest compassion possible.

I understand that what has damaged my side is not going to be taken away. The rottenness of certain past events is not going to be changed. The Gardener wants to teach me how to work with it all to create something new. It will always be dirty work. At times it will be hard work. It will cause me pain. I may stink with muck and sweat. But it will be his work, and so will eventually bring forth beauty and fragrance for someone somewhere who will see his glory in it.

◈ ◈ ◈

October 19, 19:46
To: **John; Ruth**
Subject: **box**

'You can complain because the rosebush has thorns, or you can rejoice because the thorn-bush has a rose. It's all up to you.'

Shit heap or manure pile? Hmm, well when it's got quite big, it needs forking over to let in light and air. It's a dirty job. Ultimately, of course, its purpose is to be spread around the garden, gently worked in with a trowel here and there, particularly on the barren areas that are struggling with poor soil, where there is potential for new growth with the right sustenance. In that way, what is rotten becomes enriching, not to itself but to that which it originally came from.

Penny

A weekend away at a puppetry festival has made me realise afresh my continuing difficulty with eating. My weight has dropped below the 'underweight' line after a stormy week, and I can't bring it back up again. I may have to consider some help if this goes on for much longer.

I feel I hang within my daily life by a fraying thread. It has become extremely important to me to attend church, to be at both morning and evening services. I have to be there; I have to hear God's word; I have to meet God there. It's often painful, but I believe it's important just to show up. God is my main source of hope. I have to keep standing before him, to demonstrate my need of him.

At the same time, and with equal intensity, I'm unable to deal with contact with people, even at a distance. So I have taken to spending services upstairs in the balcony alone, where my hands can give full expression to God without distracting others. Generally I'm unseen, except for John and the musicians at the front below, of whom – reassuringly – Michael is often one. I am safe here. They avert their direct gaze but I am in their peripheral vision. I am fragile, fearful that I will too easily fall apart or that others will see through my excruciatingly thin facade. I cannot bear for that to happen, so I hide even as I seek God.

◈ ◈ ◈

October 27, 05:04
To: **Ruth; John**
Subject: **box**

Hi,

If I were to say that I was not managing my eating well enough – even when spiritually / emotionally much more positive – what would be your suggestions for help with that?

Peppy

Our trio are met to talk and pray at the manse today, a detached house a mile or so from the town centre. We settle into the lounge with mugs of coffee. I briefly scan the room, taking in the evidence of family life – numerous photos in frames, a stack of DVDs, birthday cards on the mantelpiece. An armchair has been pulled around so that it's alongside another chair and the sofa, and we face each other on three sides of a square. Sunlight streams through the window.

I have no pictures today. I do have a sense of peace and stillness. We take this as meaning that I am to 'wait', that this is a pause in proceedings. After some quiet prayer we transition into a conversation about what has been happening for me. Reference is made to my eating issues and to the self-harming. I avoid addressing either topic. I still have a sense of grossness about that part of my body, both in terms of mass and repulsiveness. I am aware that it's about what is within, and not to do with how I appear to other people.

As a child I would draw my side in until the actual point of contact – the touch that was sickening, horrifying, disgusting. And then I was paralysed. Whatever happened after that was beyond my control. My inability to act was also disgusting.

I do mention my concerns about the impact that all this is having now on my relationship with Michael. There are no arguments or upsets between us, but I know I must not take his forbearance for granted. Talking about the various stresses and how his quirky but steady character interplays with the events we are managing is welcome. My marriage is an unusual pairing and one that we are growing into. We have learned how we can balance, complement and affirm each other, learned to appreciate and build our God-given union. I love him deeply and cherish this husband of mine. In the staccato moments when I have been able to relay outline updates of what is happening in relation to the prayer ministry, I have asked him how he sees things – to which his constant response is that he believes God is in control and so it will all come right. He is concerned for me in the immediate sense but unperturbed about any wider injury. He is a patient, steady and faithful man, for which I am most grateful. However, I remain aware of the fine line there may be between trusting God for the unfolding of all this, and of it testing Michael unreasonably. We acknowledge the importance of affection being expressed in such times. John and Ruth pray with me for Michael, and for the protection of our marriage.

13: In freefall

Journal entries – late October to November of Year 1

I am sitting downstairs in a pew, not in the balcony any more, feeling my place restored to me, engaging in the morning service. John has asked a question and is moving up and down the aisles to allow people's responses to be picked up on the roving microphone. The question: 'Which of you had a visitor last week? Did you feel the need to clear up for them?'

I smile quietly. I feel delighted and privileged inside, knowing that the Gardener had called and that, no, I didn't clear up. It was an unexpected visit. But anyway, it didn't bother me what state I was in. I knew he'd come to see me just as I was. He had wounds on his body, and he understood mine. And he'd been wearing his work clothes, ready to muck in alongside me.

I realise how much rage I have been projecting onto John. What I have experienced through this displacement has been forceful and frightening – out of proportion, barely controlled and as though not of me.

In reality, way back then when the abuse was happening, I was only once really physically violent in response to what was happening to me. It was sudden, out of my control and shocking. It gave short term relief from a specific situation, but was a bittersweet way to close my submission to childhood abuse. I now see how many more times in life my mute passivity had denied the 'no' screaming within me, and how much the unexpressed horror had accumulated and eventually erupted... so many times when I felt that my 'no' led to costly consequences. Confusingly, my failure to say 'no' had often also cost me dear.

November draws to a close. Today we meet again in the vestry. Ducking under some scaffolding that swathes the side wall of the church while some building work is undertaken, I let myself in through a side door for which I have a key. I want to avoid the walk through the coffee shop. Even brief glances are stressful and pretence of amiability is beyond me now, so I keep out of sight.

There is warmth and gentle concern for me as we settle in. I bat away a veiled enquiry about my wellbeing, determined to press on solely with what God might have for me today. I have to find a way to move forward.

The picture I see has been on pause from the previous time. I am still rooted at the bottom of the staircase, the ominous presence bearing down from the top landing. I am so disconcerted. This is going nowhere, it's more like a backwards step. I have not managed to reach the attic, I have not even stayed on the landing. How can I ever deal with the box in the attic?

I repeatedly try to move at least one step up, but to no avail. What courage I have is not sufficient. I grow increasingly disheartened, frustrated. I am exasperated with my own sense of failure and with the seeming pointlessness of it all. On and on, the hindrance continues.

Ruth seems to be excusing herself. I feel in a sort of limbo, split by this interruption between the picture and the events in the room. She has a funeral to conduct and is at real risk of being late. She tries to call the funeral director on his mobile but finds it's switched off, and she's trying not to let her anxiety be too apparent. She apologises and hurries away. I try to hold some semblance of composure, though I am floundering.

John begins to pray for the situation I am in, but is interrupted by a crashing sound. He heads out the door to investigate. I hear him go through into the church sanctuary and decide to follow. At the far end he is staring in dismay at the sound desk and the leaded window behind it. There is water around the window ledge and over the desk, a jagged hole in the single paned glass. I try to make sense of his words about builders sandblasting. He tries to find cloths to mop up the desk as quickly as possible, but then his mobile phone rings.

Back in the vestry we try to return to prayer. But soon he is explaining that he is now overdue to lead the midweek hymn service in the upstairs halls. I opt to stay within the confines of the room and wait, to try to compose myself. John gives me a key to lock the door from the inside for a sense of security, and assures me he will return soon.

I feel dreadful, in shaky isolation. While I understand the need for both Ruth and John to leave so abruptly, I struggle to cope with feeling so utterly alone and almost cut off from God. I wait, adrift and alone, on choppy waves.

On his return he checks my readiness to leave, and I walk in a daze to my car. At home I retreat to my room.

Today I am drawn again to Psalm 103, written by David, which talks of our youth being 'renewed like the eagles'… strong, beautiful, restored and triumphant. But this time I stop and re-read it more intently. What does it mean – exactly? I look for understanding in a Bible commentary. It describes the moulting process that birds go through, during which time the creature is vulnerable, appearing reduced, messy and weak. Once new plumage has grown, the bird's renewed strength and beauty are displayed, its power restored. I take encouragement from this illustration. I am bedraggled in my own way. I do not yet have the benefit of the new season's growth.

14: Towards Elim

Journal entries – late October to November of Year 1

I have a strong urge to anoint myself with oil.

I am at home alone. I am flummoxed by this impulse and question God. Surely it's something that someone does to or for you? I'm not supposed to do it for myself, am I? Is this right? Necessary?

But the drive increases over the day and I find I must carry it out, regardless of proper convention.

My wounds are raw and becoming unpleasant. The rot is in keeping with what I feel is inside, but it's hard to look down at myself. There is both the desire to be rid of the flesh and grief over it.

I begin to pray. I worship the God who created me, praising him for who he is and what he does, for all he has done for me. A flood of remorse and yearning washes over me. I tell him I'm so sorry for what I have done, for marring this body that he created and blessed me with. I ask for his help. I give him my commitment in moving forward – for my wounded side, with everything I have found difficult to face, for my life ahead.

I take a bottle of perfumed oil, pour it liberally into my palm. I tell God that I will honour him, I will hold his shield firmly over my vulnerable areas. I consecrate myself to him. I pour more oil into my hand and smother the side of my body in it. It glistens. Rivulets trickle towards my hip. I thank him.

◈ ◈ ◈

I wake this morning and notice that there is no discomfort on my side. As soon as I am alone, I raise my nightwear and look down. My side has healed!

The sermon at this morning's service is based on part of Exodus 15, and the parallels with my own journey stand out. Like the wandering people of Israel, from the desert of Shur I have been through Marah – doubting and grumbling, a place of bitterness. Now I am at Elim, camped by the water. This is a place of God's generous provision. I'm here, maybe a little more trusting and humble now, waiting and with a sense of calm anticipation. It's a good and safe position.

During the evening service there is time for anointing with oil. This doesn't happen very often, so I'm astonished when this is announced, so soon after my own anointing this week. I go forward. I ask God to give me all he has for me, whatever it takes.

I have been able to show Ruth my healed body. We marvel at how my skin has cleared, at God's restoration and covering of that part of me.

When I made those wounds, it was to burn off the fingermarks. Looking in the mirror today – really looking – I thought that the small marks left in their place looked like the stains of teardrops splashed down on me. Out of ugliness comes a tender, bittersweet beauty. I remember how God must grieve for the pain we inflict on each other and ourselves, and how much he also understands of what it is to be on the receiving end of it all. Tears can be releasing and healing.

I have confessed to Ruth and John that recently I had vividly visualised completely ripping from my side a large piece of flesh with my left hand, while my right hand fought to claim my armour of God – especially the breastplate and shield. I could actually see the flesh being flung across the room, splatting satisfyingly on the floor. The urge to do this was so strong, the tension between the temptation and the resistance enormous.

We re-read together the Ephesians verses about God's armour and I feel like I am fighting back.

I am unsure how to handle a new sense of wanting to weep… not to weep in shame or fear anymore, but a new kind of grief, both personal and broader. I am unsettled when these emotions rise up. I don't want to burst the banks, to cause a flood that washes away the precious and good feelings so newly held in the space God has made for me. I ask Ruth and John how I should handle it. They say it's okay, that I should go with the grief, and that's a relief. They assure me that it's not self-pity, but a reaction to keeping a lid on my anger and grief for so long. This jumble of emotions has been repressed for years. Now the new release is allowing me to be more myself, with my natural emotions surfacing. This too is part of the healing. I am deeply reassured.

I am woken in the early hours with very disturbing memories about incidents from my early adulthood… not something I had anticipated.

In my early teens, after a little over four years, my stepfather's direct abuse of me stopped, following a sudden, forceful confrontation. He was unsure if I would 'tell' on him. I was unsure if he would retaliate. There was a tense stand-off. Later, labelled 'uncontrollable', I was put into foster care. This felt like a punishment for something that was my fault. Saying no just once ultimately proved costly. I was rejected.

Some time afterwards, I was taken advantage of by a man who may well have interpreted my acquiescence to his advances as consent. It didn't occur to me to say no, to resist. I just didn't believe that saying no was a viable option. It seemed safer to be amenable to whatever he wanted.

Later again, in early adulthood, I was seriously and intimately assaulted by someone in a position of authority – an older man. This time the emphatic no I tried to give was totally disregarded. He challenged me shortly after as to whether I was going to tell, whether I would be going to the police. My response – saying no – somehow bound me to silence on it. When there was a threat of the assault being repeated, I made a sudden decision. I reasoned that it was better to go along with – to choose, even – a liaison with this man, to be consenting, and indeed even proactive, rather than be a victim again. An active, physical relationship began… shallow, tawdry and ignoble.

Perversely, it felt at the time as though going along with him gave me some control about what was happening to me rather than just being subjected to it. But my complicity produced in me a deep sense of guilt and shame, even though I maintained a brash front.

My complicity as a child had been passive. Now I knew myself to be deeply flawed, as my complicity this time felt active.

Out of the blue, I am confronted by all this, as if God wants me to face up to it. I had thought that all the work I needed to go through was to do with my childhood. But now we are in this other area.

I feel I'm losing my foothold again. Why am I being re-visited by this? What might God be wanting to teach me? It feels cruel. And I'm confused. While I'm trying to move forward in healing, everything's unravelling, as it seems that time and time again in my past I have made horrendously wrong responses.

I disclose to John and Ruth, but it shakes me to the core.

Part of me deeply regrets this speaking out, exposing it all, telling John and Ruth what I did. I hate that it's now known and I can't take that back. Another bit of me clings to the moments that followed, of God's love and acceptance. But why do I feel so wretched now? That's not honouring the blessing God gave me.

Something in me says that God must be able to heal my shame. It cannot be outside of his love and power. I will not believe it to be hopeless. God cannot have done this to cause me suffering or harm for no good purpose.

'No temptation has overtaken you except what is common to mankind. And God is faithful; he will not let you be tempted beyond what you can bear. But when you are tempted he will also provide a way out so you can endure it.' That's the Word of God (1 Corinthians 10:13). The Greek word for 'temptation' is also 'testing', which may be right here. I notice the word 'endure' – which doesn't suggest a quick fix. But there is the promise of a 'way out'. How or when, though?

I'm so tired and wonder if I am on my own from here.

15: The angels on the landing

Journal entries – late October to November of Year 1

I am in the depths. I spend many hours secretly in the church sanctuary, appealing to God for an understanding of why I am visited by additional past shame. I read and re-read Ephesians 6 – the armour of God passage – and Psalm 139, which reminds me of how intimately I am known to God. And Psalm 62, which helps me voice my reaching out to God.

Alone in the sanctuary, I am wrung out before God. I choose to believe that God is here with me, understands. And finally there is a quiet knowing, a whispered assurance: 'I am with you in this.' That's all that matters for now.

At the end of three turbulent days, the tenderness with which I feel God coming alongside me, tending to my pain and twisted self-image, is intensely quiet. I understand now how God wants access to this other part of my story, the true basis of which I have always kept secret. It's never been secret from him, of course. He wants me to give him access there. He wants to teach me that he still loves me, he can still renew me. I am beautiful and precious in his sight.

It's later and I'm lying in bed thinking about the question, 'Why was God not there when the bad stuff happened?' Gently, I come to thinking that he *was* there. Why didn't he intervene? I don't know.

I realise I have found it hard to consider him 'there'... knowing and seeing what happened. I have felt outrage about that, and shame. I have to choose to submit it all to him and allow him to deal with it. He's always loved me. Stuff happens. He waits, able to use it for good. Shit happens. He waits, able to turn it into manure.

I am due to meet John and Ruth this morning. Quite how we all have such certainty that what's going on is in God's will and direction is beyond me. But our mutual conviction remains.

In the weak light of the early morning I trudge across the field with Daisie, whose dark eyes and drooped posture reflect the gloom of both my mood and the weather. Neither of us like the drizzle that began after we set off, so maybe we will curtail our route. The horses in the paddock stand motionless by the water trough as Daisie and I cross. The wooden stile is wet and mossy, and my boot slips momentarily as I negotiate it. Daisie has pushed through alongside me so I hold the rickety post and lean back a little so she can complete her manoeuvre, then I follow her. Just a few steps on and there is the next stile to negotiate. I hold back this time and allow Daisie to hurdle through, then make my way over, more laborious and heavy-footed than she is.

Daisie has picked up a scent and snuffles intently around the grass. She senses so much of what is unseen through markers and signals of which I have no perception or knowledge. I quietly marvel at how much of this world is beyond the scope of our awareness or experience; how much we can miss without careful attendance; how limited we are. Yet we are so special in this created order.

Daisie follows the invisible trail. I let out the lead and make my way behind and beside her as she explores the direction it takes her. The gate tucked in the old hedgerow comes into view. 'Come. This way.'

A couple of hours later John and Ruth greet me with anticipation and delight. It's been a challenging few weeks. They share my relief and joy over the picture of the Gardener, but we are all concerned about the ongoing turbulence. John and Ruth pray, then quieten as I focus on asking God to reveal his will for me now, to show me how to proceed. We praise, we wait, we seek. The picture unfolds. Bottom of the staircase again. I resolve not to allow myself to become despondent. I determine to trust. Deadlock. I am desperate to move against the forces holding me back, and to face my fears. Over and over I will my foot to step up, only to be paralysed. I am exhausted, close to the end of my resources. I pray for help.

Ruth is reading a Bible passage and I hear her speak of angels and that 'nothing will be able to separate us from the love of God.'

Nothing will be able to separate me. I hear her read it again: 'neither life nor death, neither angels nor demons, neither the present time nor the future, nor any powers, neither height nor depth, nor anything else in all creation, will be able to separate us from the love of God that is in Christ Jesus our Lord.'

In my picture, I am suddenly surrounded by angels as I stand at the bottom of those stairs.

'I have angels all around me!' I say. These are strong protectors. I am buoyed by their protective shield. And there are so many!

'Can you go up the stairs?' I hear from John.

'No, I can't move through,' I reply. I am hemmed in by these wonderful beings. I am enormously relieved by their presence, but aware of some frustration at my remaining static. I bask in their encircling care, yet know that ultimately I have to get up those stairs and deal with what repels me so.

'There are too many angels!' John exclaims, exasperated. 'This needs to be scaled down so you can get through!'

What am I meant to do? And then I hear it, I hear the list of the 'armour of God' being read out by Ruth.

'Read it again. Slowly.' I hear each item listed. 'Read it again.'

'Put on the full armour of God… Stand firm… with the belt of truth buckled around your waist, with the breastplate of righteousness in place, and with your feet fitted with the readiness that comes from the gospel of peace… take up the shield of faith, with which you can extinguish all the flaming arrows of the evil one. Take the helmet of salvation and the sword of the

Spirit, which is the word of God…'

I visualise each item as literal armour strapped onto me. I have faith that these things represent what is provided by a most loving and generous God. I hold to my belief that he can equip me as I need. I push back my own inadequacy.

In a moment, once I am fully equipped, the angels suddenly move aside. They have not left me. There are still as many there. But now they line each side of the stairs instead of being gathered around me. A way has opened through the middle of them. There is just enough room for me to get by if I choose.

One step at a time… one slow, hard, step by step.

I raise each foot in turn and place it down. I am going up the stairs. The concentration and effort is intense, but I am making way with a continual silent naming and sensing of all my protective equipment.

The last, top step. I fight my fear of what has been waiting there. I turn and will myself to look. In that instant, I see that it is gone.

'I'm on the landing.' I inform John and Ruth. 'The landing is *mine*.'

16: Growing and dreaming

Emails and journal entries – End October to January of Year 2

October 28, 14:05
To: **John; Ruth**
Subject: **box**

I was so relieved not to have to describe the scene that I was avoiding at the top of the stairs. However, having overcome, it has occurred to me that there is a certain amount of upside-down ribald humour in the way it was dealt with... weapons and swords... Not sure if God intended that, but it's making me smile anyway, which is pretty bloody fantastic!

And I've just had lunch :) Thank you so much, Peppy

October 28, 16:56
To: **John; Ruth**
Subject: **box**

This is *really* not a spiritual response but I'm sure you can cope with it. There's a lot that's not of my normal self at the moment and here's another bit... Today is like looking at a little piece of my past in the face and saying, 'Er, *no* actually – f*** *YOU*!' I quite like that piece of not normal.

Peppy

I have been calm since the last session, with a sense of being hedged around, shielded. I have put the 'armour of God' verses on my mobile so I can easily remind myself of them. I can't seem to take in anything else for now. As John says, I need to 'stay with the moment.' I am exhausted yet enormously relieved and grateful to have reached some point of overcoming.

I've received an email from a friend who emigrated a few years ago. I miss her passion and colour. Like me, she's a very visual person and that helps us relate. In the letter she mentions something that happened about ten years ago. She writes, 'I remember God giving me a picture of you. You asked me to draw it for you and I tried but it turned out rubbish, so I was too scared to give it to you. It was a picture of you hiding in a dark room, peeping out through a crack in some heavy double doors, into a room filled with light and wonderful things. But you wouldn't go through. You just agonised behind the door, somehow not believing that what was laid out in the other room was for you.'

I had forgotten about that, and she's not aware of what I am dealing with here, so the timing of her bringing it up again is remarkable. I am comforted by the reminder of there being light ahead and wonderful things prepared for me. In my heart I hold these things in trust.

It's going to be a good Christmas. I find it easier by the day to eat reasonably normally, and to relax in company. I am looking forward to a new year with softer horizons ahead.

Last year was a year of descent. At times, it was descent almost into an abyss. 'If I go down to the depths you are there' (Psalm 39). It's not just poetry. I have lived it.

My heart rests in the opening verses of Isaiah 40: 'I waited patiently for the Lord; He turned to me and heard my cry. He lifted me out of the slimy pit, out of the mud and mire; He set my feet on a rock, He gave me a firm place to stand. He put a new song in my mouth, a hymn of praise to our God. Many will see and fear and put their trust in the Lord.'

Each realisation of how Jesus has cleaned and healed another bit of me is wonderful. It's like professional cleaners have been into my house. To start with, so much dust and dirt was kicked up, so many grotty nooks and crannies exposed. Suddenly the furniture is back in place, the surfaces shine and cupboards are tidy. A glance round brings delight that this is a place where visitors may feel welcome and comfortable. But – note to self! – daily housework is still necessary, even following a spring clean!

Last night I was praying, thanking God for the present time of peace and security. Though calm, I anticipate another change coming up. I have a sense of impending movement, of the need to be ready. I feel undaunted, even eager. I pray for the situations of family estrangement in my life and ask for direction. I feel I can ask for a task that's big enough that – without God – failure is guaranteed.

January 9, 08:31
To: **John; Ruth**
Subject: **Ready**

Hi,

Just so you know, last night I had a clear sense of God telling me, 'Be ready, we're about to move on from here.' I was reminded of the point in Jehoshaphat's story of the pause before the march towards the pass. I had a picture of one of those men reclining on the ground, with all his equipment, weapons and provisions around him – not discarded, just loosely to hand while he rested. As the instruction came to stand up and make ready, he gradually got up and put back all those things firmly about him, then stood on his feet, waiting for the call to move forward. Then I had in mind the Exodus story, of the Israelites staying in the desert while God supplied all they needed until he told them to move on.

I've no idea what comes next but I'm ready to walk on.

Penny

There's been a delay in the next get together with John and Ruth. Part of me wants to press on, knowing I'll be missing out on further blessing if I don't. Part of me wants to draw back. Why wade back into the shit heap now I've got my posh frock and high heels on?

January 22, 08:10
To: **John; Ruth**
Subject: **dream**

I just told Michael about a dream I've had, and I thought I'd tell you too. I knew during the dream that it was from God and I wrote it down straightaway.

I was ushered in to see someone. They were lying in a hospital bed in a lounge in a home. The person who ushered me in was anxious about coping with who was in the bed, and their situation, and the closeness of their death. The person in bed was distressed. I leaned over them, sitting on the side of the bed. They reached to my face, slapping and pushing it. I remained still. The first person stepped forward to intervene. I put my hand out to stop them. I understood I needed to allow and absorb the lashing out. It wasn't personal. I stroked their face and allowed them to touch mine, alternately caressing and slapping me.

I asked 'How is it for you?' The person in the bed knew I was fully paying attention to them, caring for them.

I asked, 'How may I help you?'

Attention was locked on, touch continued. Their agitation eased.

I asked, 'May I speak to God about you?' Non-verbal assent was given.

I asked, 'May I introduce you to God?' Non-verbal assent was given. I did so in spirit, watching as they met God. I stayed physically, but stepped back within.

Peace came to the person. They died in peace.

I believe this is an illustration of how God wants me to minister to others, how I am to serve him. I don't know who the person in the bed represents... whether a particular individual, or people generally that I am to be alongside as a 'wounded healer'. I think it's the manner, or template, of how to treat them that's what matters most. Not new. But I guess anything that confirms a calling must be good!

Peppy

I receive positive responses from John and Ruth about my dream. They say they get a clear sense of me in the dream and consider my interpretation of it is correct. Yes, it's what we knew already, but God often says the same things several times because it helps us deal with doubt later. It may help me put a little more flesh on the bones of my gifting.

17: Towards Easter

Emails and journal entries – January to March of Year 2

January 23, 08:46
To: **John; Ruth**
Subject: **open box**

I know there's an oddness in me. What I don't know is why or what for, other than God seems to indicate to me that it's how he's made me. Yet I'm not always comfortable when aware that some people perceive an odd side of me, and I have to fight against trying to appear more conventional. But I can't bear the thought of losing any part of God's work in and through me, so suppressing that side of me is not really an option. The sense of isolation is sometimes hard.

I tell Michael everything. He cannot relate to it, yet is the one person who completely accepts and affirms it all, marvellous man that he is – and odd in his own way, too!

Peppy

At the church Burns Night party I see a woman who'd upset me so much last summer that she's assumed the form of a monster to me. I've avoided her ever since, pleading inside that she wouldn't approach me, as I wasn't sure I could trust my heart or tongue in response.

What had happened? Well, this woman gave a talk at a meeting which unexpectedly focussed on dealing with childhood abuse. At the time it simply hadn't been helpful or encouraging to me. I felt from what she had said that there was a danger that I would always be internally damaged by what had happened. I was repelled by the prospect, distressed by my feelings towards her.

But now, in the dancing, suddenly she's in the line of people moving forward to the line I'm in. As I look at her, I see her differently. With compassion. I'm reminded of a TV ad where a woman walks out of her house followed by the shadow of a dragon looming up behind her. When the light shifts, the shadow becomes a child in a dressing up costume and it's all different.

This is all part of God's healing work in me – and I can pray that it is in her too.

Walking with Daisie and Jesus these chill mornings, I contemplate the fallen leaves. In the autumn, they were firm in form, distinct in colour and shape, lying on top of the ground. Now they have largely disintegrated, merging, absorbed into the ground-scape. In time they will fertilise the soil, providing nutrients for new growth. The old is not wasted; it's transformed and part of the renewal.

Today there's another meeting at the manse with my two companions on the way. It's a positive and affirming time and we're all sure the time is coming to move on. We agree that I should compile my story for giving as a talk at church at some point. We discuss how it would best be presented, agreeing that having John and Ruth either side of me to prompt me with questions and support me through any gaps that my nerves may open up would be best.

During this session there is another flashback to my youth to disclose, and new difficulty with food has surfaced, which I think is all related to the forgiveness and healing. I feel upset that the whole eating issue is back. It's been such a delight and relief the last few weeks to have ease on it. The last few weeks have perhaps been more respite than final chapter. There's no point in being resentful.

I need to press on. I have learned that things are not always what they seem. I may never get full insight or explanation on my past. The sad and painful possibility that this has all been born out of a lack of love and protection in my life does not define my worth. First and foremost, I am God's child.

February – and Elly's birthday has not gone as she had hoped. Last night she went with a group of new friends from college to a mate's band gig in the next town. Unfortunately, one girl arrived drunk and Elly felt obliged to spend most of the evening with her in the toilets while she sat on the floor giggling, shrieking or vomiting. She also felt obliged to follow her when she went running across the field in the dark. Elly was dismayed that the other girls thought the whole thing funny and wouldn't help at all. Then there was a scary taxi ride back home in falling snow, by which time Elly was in tears. After food, four of the girls stay for a sleepover, all packed like sardines into her bedroom, but they wake early and begin chatting loudly. Elly goes off to the spare room in a resentful strop. I dole out juice, croissants and bacon baguettes regardless of the birthday girl's absence and wave them off cheerily as their parents' cars pull into the drive.

Later, I send Elly and George off to the local hill with a couple of old trays to sledge on, while I cook a comforting spaghetti bolognese. I'm undecided how much red wine should go in the food and how much in my glass.

Meanwhile, we've reached a milestone with George. He's had a musical epiphany. Last week he told me in astonishment that he's discovered how cool Indie is, and actually he's starting to find that the hard metal he's been into for the last couple of years is a bit repetitive. Hallelujah! Then yesterday he came home from school to announce that he'd unexpectedly gone to the jazz band rehearsal at lunchtime – and loved it! So the era of the rock-gods practising in our home most weekends may be drawing to a close. That's ambrosia to my soul. Beethoven by this time next year?

A clear prompt from this morning's sermon causes me to make a phone call as soon as I get home, giving an unexpected and unprecedented invitation to someone long estranged to come for a meal with the family. I have called my mother. I walk into the lounge and casually mention what I've done, and count the many seconds of astonished silence from my family as they take in the news. 'Well done,' they tell me.

The appointed day for the milestone visit comes. Today, for the first time in my adult life, my mother comes to visit me, to have lunch. It's always been a distant and uneasy relationship, fractured badly by my time in care.

I start to panic when she and her husband of these later years arrive half an hour early, while Michael is still out getting a jar of coffee. But Daisie's bounding welcome takes much of the attention. I busy myself putting the kettle on and preparing the mugs until Michael returns, which brings its own distraction to the scene. There is superficial chitchat, but I am able to make eye contact and engage in short bits of conversation. I make a generous lunch to give as best I can in that way, leaning into the reassuring motions of hospitality.

Inwardly, I repeatedly turn my attention to my framed aide-memoire on the wall: 'Thus far the Lord has helped me, so I can trust him for what is ahead.' I try to be anchored, calmed.

It's odd to look across at this elderly woman sitting on my sofa, mild and benign, talking about bird-watching and gardening. I recognise her, yet don't know her. You would never guess this was the same woman who caused me so much pain all those years ago. I realise how much freer I am of the awful crippling burden this had previously been to me. I find I am able to see her differently now, with glances of grace, catching the ordinariness that characterises her. I ponder the knowledge that she is – like me – very precious to her Creator God, even if she is unaware of it.

Nothing much changes as far as what I mean to her is concerned, but I am fairly at ease with that. She is as she is. The big difference lies in my truly knowing that I am God's child, and that is where my identity and security are now firmly set. That gives a perspective and takes precedence. I accept that a certain pang of grief may remain within me, but the comfort and security God offers dulls the sting.

I felt in the lead up to this day a sense that I must just be present and hospitable. Simple, though enormously challenging. But, with God, I have been able to be both those things, quietly and well, allowing another bit of healing to be done, in me at least.

18: Easter comes

Journal entries – March to April of Year 2

I want to honour God in telling my story at church and have spent careful time on it. It's a matter of weeks away now. I feel doubtful and inadequate one moment, strong in my faith and resolve the next. Keeping focussed on his will is like trying to listen for seagulls' cries in the face of a tsunami. Can I carry this through?

My companions and I are working to assemble an evening service to tell the story. Ruth has recently run a series at her church called 'Real people, real lives, real God' and since this is to be a joint service between the two churches, we advertise it under that banner, but it's to be hosted at my church. We meet to discuss and decide how to present it all, concluding that a loose Q&A format between us, with accompanying pictures on the screen – Dani's illustrations of my pictures of the box in the attic – will work best.

We spend some hours together at the manse, lunch spread on a wooden garden table in the spring sunshine, bringing order to the events of the last year or so.

I am finding it difficult to consider exposing some of the detail, but know that the glory of God's work in the mess to bring me towards restoration will only be fully apparent if I am open and honest about my brokenness. I'm apprehensive about the prospect of speaking publicly, of letting go what I have kept secret and hidden. But I really want to let God's healing have centre stage.

This evening, Easter Sunday, I sit between John and Ruth facing a packed church and, heart pounding, I unpack my story of what God has done for me. I conclude by saying that I had not fully recognised quite how shackled I had been before, but God knew and God wanted me to be truly free. Nothing put into God's hands is wasted. He can pour his light and love into even the most desperately dark places. I retain the memories of the bad experiences, together with a new understanding of the damaging effects on me – emotionally, mentally, and spiritually. But I am now freed from the crippling burden put on me by fear and shame. There will continue to be sensitive spots, tender scars. But no open wounds. I am learning to forgive both those who directly acted wrongly against me, I add, and to forgive those who did nothing about it – something which is already profoundly liberating.

I say all this. Then, shaking, I take my seat next to Michael, and John and Ruth continue with the communion service. I sense in my spirit a voice saying, 'Well done.' It is done.

For the ten days since my talk I have been feeling gloriously buoyed, and relieved that it's all behind me. Many people who were at my talk have taken to calling me Peppy… not something I actually asked for, but it's delightful to have it offered.

Yes, I've had moments of doubt and derision, questioning the purpose of sharing my story publicly. Occasionally I am anxious about whether the telling of my story benefitted anyone at all, whether God was able to use it for good. Ruth assures me that he has and will do, but reminds me that I may well never personally be made fully aware of how that is. I must trust that into his hands alone.

God has given me a picture today. I am standing in my kitchen holding some large beads in my hands. These seem to have been a necklace of some sort, but the string has been cut. I know this had been around my neck, but is no more. Suddenly my hands jolt and all the beads scatter on the floor, rolling away out of sight under my kitchen units. I panic. I fall on my knees, scrabbling for them. But they've all disappeared.

I then feel, 'Get up, and leave them. You don't have to find them. I know where they are and will deal with them in time.'

I think this is what God is showing me about how to deal with what has happened to my story now.

I *am* becoming steadily stronger. My confidence has grown. I am moving on from the disturbance and discomfort that came through the prayer ministry and my talk at church. There is a joy in me, founded on such gratitude for how God lovingly took me through it all, from his desire to have me more healed and whole. I am lighter and freer now, released. I have a greater freedom to praise and worship God unfettered.

A few days before Dani and I go on a long weekend away with a group of friends, she has an idea for a sketch for our puppets which she storyboards for me on some scrap A4 paper. It uses the analogy of a mountain to climb. Someone has a call from God to go up the mountain but takes their own baggage with them. God's voice coaxes them to put it down, to let him hold it all, but they do not easily concede. They become defeated and disheartened, but then a helper comes alongside who throws the baggage into a pile before them. The person then resumes climbing easily – and a sunset reveals the silhouette of a cross built into the precipice.

The sketch starts further ideas sparking between us, and the mountain morphs into a funfair setting with various rides depicting the challenging experiences of life. It quickly develops into a draft production – ten scenes in all. We make the main character, possibly in a tatty patchwork style, someone carrying a backpack. A second character keeps appearing in different guises – ticket-seller, caretaker, guide or ride-operator. This bemuses the main character who asks, 'Haven't I met you somewhere before?' Through the action, dialogue and lyrics, the main character is confronted with the choice of whether to trust this guide or not. A number of funfair rides portray his experiences, representing the sometimes unsettling process of 'unpacking before God' and giving him charge of it all – past, present, and future. One scene has a mysterious box being opened Pandora-like, with dreadful forces flying out, as from a haunted house. We return to that scene towards the end, and have the main character discover that all that is left in the bottom of the box is hope.

The main character is finally made strong and well – now sewn neatly together, though the scars are discernible. He's healed, whole and with real hope. We consider titling the production 'Not Fair' but for now give it a working title of 'Out of the Box' as a nod to the inspiration drawn from my own life. We hope that one day resources will allow us to stage this as a full scale production. For now we cherish the fun and delight of being creative.

With Easter behind me, I have my low days. Ruth refers me to Mary Magdalene, who is the first one chosen to see the resurrected Jesus. Even resurrection appearances, fleeting and wondrous, were no guarantee of difficulties being over, she says. Peter's ministry, for example, was not a bellyfull of laughs. But what they did know was that Christ was alive and with them.

I am told not to have regrets. She assures me that she does not think less of me for all I have told her. She says it took guts to share what I did and she's not surprised I'm tired. I should not be afraid of the brokenness. Joy is not annulled by accompanying fears and confusion. There was still fear on Easter Sunday.

'Instead of your shame you will receive a double portion, and instead of disgrace you will rejoice in your inheritance. And so you will inherit a double portion in your land, and everlasting joy will be yours.'

I feel today I can believe and hold onto this promise from Isaiah 61. I know that when Mary Magdalene stood weeping and reeling in the garden, Jesus was not absent. When the disciples walked that road to Emmaus, he was not absent. He allowed for the full process of human experience to unfold in order to have his glory revealed. From the depths of worldly despair, they broke through to the heights of spiritual revelation.

The Chronicles of the Box

Part 2

19: In and out of control

Journal entries – September to October of Year 2

Vera, a dear friend who is a vicar, has asked me several times if I'd like to go on a pilgrimage with her to Israel. I've known her since the start of her curacy and she was a pivotal influence when the puppet team was going through a difficult patch and needed an enthusiastic push. This steady zeal characterises her well. She is dogged in faith and delightful in expressions of joy and I so love that mix. I've not been sure, though, if the Israel trip is something I want to do, and I'm doubtful it's affordable. Unexpectedly, that has all shifted in a positive way. I am indeed joining her on a tour in a few weeks. And I'm delighted that Dani has made a last minute decision to come too.

I break the news of my impending absence to Elly and George. The conversation illustrates their characters well:

P – I wondered if it would be okay with you two if I went away on a trip?

G – Yeah, okay.

E – Where? What trip? Where are you going? When is it?

P – It's a trip away with Vera and Dani.

G – Yeah, okay.

E – Where? What trip? Where are you going? When will it be?

P – Israel.

G – Israel? Yeah, okay.

E – (Shrieks) Israel! Wow!

G – Will you get murdered?

P – Well, that's no more likely that it would be here.

G – Oh, okay then.

E – Israel – wow! When are you going? How come?

P – (Explains a bit more)

E – Tell Dani I'll look after her kids for her, won't you?

P – Okay, but actually their dad and grandma have sorted most of that.

G – I won't.

E – I'll babysit after college.

G – I won't. Hey mum, look, I can do eye-farts. (Demonstrates.)

E – It's your fault you know, you brought him up.

P – I know. Sorry.

E – Where will you be going in Israel? What will you do? What will you see?

P – (Explains a bit more)

G – Cool!

E – That's amazing!

P – So, is that okay with you two?

E – Oh, yes!

G – Yeah. Hey, Mum, look, I can do slap-bass on your knee. (Demonstrates.)

P – So you'll be okay and look after each other while I'm gone?

G – Yeah. Can I give you a piggy-back to your room now?

P – No, I want to go downstairs.

G – Okay, downstairs then.

P – No, I'm too scared.

E – Mum, he's your fault, you know.

G – Come on, Mum, hop on. (Silly struggle ensues in the doorway, before I'm lifted up for the steps down.)

P – (Back on the landing) Night night, then.

I think that went well.

The brink of autumn. Michael has long wanted to experience a hot-air balloon flight. Great vistas and soaring perspectives exhilarate him. Last week he asked me if I'd like us to go on a balloon flight for my birthday. I remind him of my dislike of heights, of how my head reels to look down on any drop over ten feet. I tell him I don't think it's for me but maybe it would be a good idea for *his* birthday next year.

Later I hear him on the phone to the balloon-owner, and assume he's making apologies and a cancellation and leave him to it. I wonder if he might be disappointed, as he says nothing after the call. Nothing, that is, until last evening – when he casually asks if I'm okay to go on the balloon flight today. Apparently he discussed my situation with the balloon man and between them they decided I would be fine actually, so it was going ahead!

I am appalled at the prospect. I talk to him about how apprehensive it makes me, and add that after an emotionally difficult few months I don't think I have any spare capacity for handling any form of stress or fear. I've been working at capacity for a long time now and I don't want to add in unnecessary extras. But it's too late now. I send out texts to several friends asking them to pray for me, and soften the edges of my senses with a quantity of red wine.

I think of a hymn verse that John has shared with me: 'Ye fearful saints / fresh courage take. / The clouds ye so much dread / are filled with mercy and shall break / with blessings on your head.'

Elly and George come along to watch from the ground. I reluctantly climb into the basket and as it is loosed from its tether my head and stomach lurch with every sway and glimpse of the receding ground. Michael marvels exultantly at the wondrous panorama below us. I cling on, internally and externally, until there is a reassuring bump on terra firma again.

Gift-giving may not be Michael's forte, though I appreciate his good intentions and unalloyed delight in the world around him. I certainly envy his inner freedom.

Coming out of my church small group meeting this afternoon, when we'd been looking at the Exodus story, I bump into John. I ask him why my own 'desert journey' seems so much longer and harder than I'd originally anticipated.

He talks about the wanderings of the Israelites in the wilderness. If they had taken a shorter or more direct route they may have been confronted by the Philistines, with devastating consequences. God, he said, is not to be hurried when a short cut may be harmful to us, whether we see the threat lurking over the horizon or not. The extended period of time was also necessary to teach them, through desolation and dependency, lessons they absolutely needed to learn before being able to enter the Promised Land. God would have a particular purpose in the pace he set for my own journey, and I could trust him for that.

George comes home this evening with a baleful look on his face. Today, in his German class, everyone had to say what their parents'

jobs were. George asked what the German word for 'puppet' was. The teacher, annoyed, twice asked him why he needed to ask that. Then, in spite of his assurances that I am indeed a puppeteer, the teacher sent him out of the room, while his mates (who know what I do) doubled over laughing. She followed him out, demanding to know why he had said such a thing. He was thoroughly told off for being so silly and causing a disruption to class. He protested the legitimacy of his query and eventually – grudgingly – she let him return to the classroom.

'Yeah, well, thanks for being a puppeteer.'

Fortunately, he's laughing now – almost as much as I am.

Something has gone. I register that a piece of silent hidden rage that was deep in me has dissipated. An ease replaces it.

After a positive week, I am emotionally tripped up during conversation with two friends. They know I am going through prayer ministry, and that it's challenging. They have the sensitivity and wisdom not to ask about it, they simply offer acceptance. We sit in a warm conservatory chatting through a spectrum of both trivia and real concerns of life. It's good to be in such company, and to think of things outside myself.

Out of nowhere I feel shaken, flooded with shame. My friends continue their banter, oblivious. My anxiety focuses on a sudden conviction that I can't be at all effective in telling anything of this story for God, given how weak and vulnerable I'm prone to be.

I realise it's not over… I am going to have to go back into the house in my pictures. Though fearful of the risk to my mental health, I cannot bear to stay as I am.

I take my leave of my friends. As the saying goes, we walk up mountains but trip over pebbles. Those pebbles can be on the way down as well as the way up. I know it's better to smile as I look back at the mountain, rather than stop and stare at the stupid pebble.

There is more work, more forgiving to do, otherwise it's like trying to put on clean clothes over a grubby body. Or trying to sweep out one room while constantly treading through the muck from another. What am I trying to do? Forgive those people for who they are? For their not being prompted to respect or protect or love me? Who am I to demand that?

Meanwhile, I am discovering that 3am is not a good time to wrestle with demons, literally or figuratively. I don't doubt that God is there, but he feels at a distance. Prayer is bleak. I feel like I am leaving sticky note messages in a cubby hole for God to find later.

20: Israel

Journal entries – November of Year 2

I get back from the trip to Israel to find the family very pleased with themselves for having managed perfectly well without me. I'm impressed – until I discover they've lived on takeaways much of the time. The house is thick with dust and dog hair, apart from the centre of the lounge floor which has been hurriedly vacuumed on the day I return. No washing has been done.

Ah, well, I'm glad they muddled along happily together, and they're so pleased to have me back. I'm trying to be grateful that Elly came to no harm when she had a minor incident on her new moped, and not to mind that they decided not to mention it to me while I was away.

Having coffee after the morning service the next day, I find it increasingly hard to keep coming up with jolly pat phrases when people ask how it was for Dani and me in Israel. I know it's perfectly natural and reasonable for people to ask, though mostly they only really want a quick 'amazing / fantastic / great, thanks...' But it seems trite and ridiculous to keep answering that way.

Then someone starts grilling me, firing questions – had I done this or done that? But not allowing me to say exactly what I had done. Thankfully someone interrupts us. The hubbub itself reminds me of how I felt in Jerusalem – cluttered, confused and sometimes overwhelmed, with so much to absorb that I wasn't able to process then and there. The truth is, I still feel full to overflowing and actually quite dazed, and that's leaving me with no reserves of grace towards others. Clearly, I've not returned all glowing with joy and pre-Christmas sparkle. I'm deeply affected, yet it's hard to express properly yet, or to move seamlessly back into normal life. I feel like a deeper layer of my spirit has been opened up, one I'm not familiar with yet, and it's still somewhat raw and sensitive. I know God will help me deal with it all in time. I feel a bit odd… not right in myself, though I can't quite identify or address it.

Thankfully we manage to have the afternoon to ourselves as family, talking about my time away and getting out all the bits and bobs I'd bought.

So, how to describe the trip? Many of the sites we visit, particularly in Jerusalem, aren't in themselves helpful to me – big 'bling' churches, with shrines to this, that and the other everywhere, usually presented as 'tradition has it that this is where...' Well-meaning, but simply clutter that I have to fight through, exasperatingly getting in the way of what I want to focus on. I don't miss the irony of this being so representative of how life and faith can seem or be made by us, with so much of life's clutter obscuring our view of God.

Bethlehem itself is not a lovely place. We go straight into the Church of the Nativity, a big barn of a building looking more like a fortress than a church. We shuffle forward slowly for ages in a big crowd, eventually funnelling down through a small doorway into a cave-like lower room. Here there's another bling shrine covering a hole in the floor where you can put your hand to 'touch the spot where tradition has it that Jesus was born'. I duly do this. I feel that you do these things because you're there and that's what everyone does. But none of it does anything for me, other than make me think, 'This is ridiculous really...'

Then I hear two men at the back of the room singing a worship song together, quietly. It's spine-tinglingly beautiful. I walk over to stand beside them and listen, and begin to pray. I pray and sing in sign language, praising and worshipping God for Jesus and all that his coming to Bethlehem means for us. In that moment, I am impacted with such a strong sense of God's presence, it's awesome.

It's as though the separation between the spiritual and physical worlds becomes very thin, that I am able to feel it so much more than normal. The focus is on God... God coming as a helpless vulnerable baby because he loves us so much, wants to connect with us.

There's one other woman in our group who signs. She is suddenly in front of me, saying that she feels the same. I find it difficult to speak about how it is for me, so sign instead, overwhelmed by awe and holy fear and wonder.

Then Vera is leading me out because we have to move on, but I almost can't bear the physical movement disturbing my spiritual focus. I don't want to move away, it's distressing me, even though I know the place isn't 'magic' in itself. I want to cling to his closer presence.

It takes me a while to be okay again. I still need to sign through lunch rather than talk. While I've not physically prostrated myself, I am nonetheless on my face before God. There's joy within it, but the awe is the greatest thing.

It isn't easy to tell people about it, though… not without sounding super-spiritual. And it isn't as though there's a specific point to the experience. Yet I know it wasn't simply a surge of peace and love in a self-indulgent 'feel good' way. I feel close to God and I think it's for the strengthening of my faith.

Equally moving is our time at the Muslim boys' home in Israel's West Bank.

The plan is for Dani and me to take the gift of one of our puppets to the home. We'd been told before the trip that the boys would not be there while we were, so we don't bother to take any props for a show.

We'd had some fun moments all through that first week, taking the puppet out here and there and taking photos of him at various sites.

When we get to the boys' home, it's all pretty basic. A senior member of staff tells us about the home, also of his own story of being one of the first boys to stay there, a few decades before. At nine years old he found himself living and being loved at this place and subsequently benefitting from a scholarship which enabled him to go to university and gain a degree. He might have used that as a springboard to escape the area and the circumstances of his boyhood, but instead chose to return and help nurture other young lives there as they too healed from experiences of violence, abuse, neglect and loss.

As we are taken back downstairs, a young boy, with obvious ease and delight, chatters brightly to this man, who rests his hand affectionately on the boy's shoulder. I am struck by the beautiful simplicity of the way this seems to model God's love, and feel moved and humbled.

We are shown the dining hall and are surprised to see boys there, after all, having lunch. We quickly get the puppet out of its bag and make it smile and wave as we are ushered through, prompting smiles and waves in return. In the adjacent room, Dani and I are suddenly asked if we'd like – just the two of us – to go and give the puppet to the boys.

We're taken to a common room where a large number of boys are watching TV. Not at all sure what to do, we make the puppet peep round the door to say hi. A cluster of young boys gather round, slightly bewildered but curious. Exclamations pop and sparkle through the doorway. Someone tells us to go to the front of the room. We're like rabbits in headlights. We are unused to working without a staging curtain to screen ourselves and kick ourselves for not bringing any props.

With the help of a translator we manage some kind of introduction and then the kids are encouraged to come forward to touch the puppet. The boys are tentative for a few moments, then suddenly we are swamped. They are touching, holding, kissing, pressing their faces onto the puppet, pulling on it, bowled over if it hugs anyone. After enough time for them to get the idea of how the puppet 'works', we know we should just let go, give it away, and so we do. We find a member of staff to hand it to, with a two-minute lesson on how to hold and operate it. Then we step back and watch the boys, all excitedly milling round.

Dani and I quietly withdraw, then have a good cry in the corridor.

We both feel so humbled. The circumstances and reactions of those boys really bring us up short. We realise that we weren't meant to do the sketch. That would have been too much for the boys to take in, all at once. And the sketch we'd had in mind – telling the story about the human tendency to rely on 'stuff' – would have been totally inappropriate for boys with almost no 'stuff' and who clearly already have God's love modelled to them in this sparse but special place.

Our last three days are spent by Galilee, a welcome contrast to Jerusalem. Here there is a natural beauty and tranquillity that restores my soul. Vera leads us in an open air communion service by the lakeside, the bright still waters behind her reflecting something of the calm and depth of this blessed ritual. Our group goes out on a boat and, as part of a short service aboard, I stand to read the passage at the end of the fourth chapter of Mark, recounting how Jesus stills a great storm while out on a boat here with his disciples. I smile within as I reflect on the storm I have been through, of his presence with me in that, and authority over it. My praise to him overflows, and I am buoyed by his benevolent love.

21: In the desert

Journal entries – December to February of Year 3

Re-engaging with my normal routine and circle of friends after the intense time in Israel is strangely difficult. I've been weepy since my return, feeling the distance in time and geography almost a form of loss. I am puzzled by this reaction, as I'm quite sure that being able to meet with God and grow in my faith and relationship with him is not dependent on proximity to a land he once walked. To be honest, I'm sceptical about the way many people have an almost superstitious reverence for the Holy Land, which goes way beyond the usefulness of appreciating something of the area and culture that Jesus inhabited. I believe that there's much that is special and spiritual there, but I'm not sure I consider it to be necessarily any closer to God's Spirit than anywhere else in his creation. Surely he is as close to me here in the middle of England as in the Middle East? And yet I gently grieve.

I have begun to feel that there are people – I'm not sure who exactly – who disdain me. Those inklings are escalating… burning more intensely each day, a spark kindling a forest fire. I sense that these people see through my cloak of respectability to the nakedness of my core degradation. What is happening?

These people, they have heard something of my story. They heard it in church at Easter, of course. They politely smile, while privately regarding me with quiet contempt. Over time, they must be becoming less concerned with disguising their attitude towards me. I have been a fool. I don't know why I thought I could possibly be rid of the stain on my soul. It has blotted me through and through and it surely defines me. They see me for what I am and they despise me.

I am in a state of constant tension. The sense of obligation to continue unpacking the box remains but I seriously question whether I can carry it out. Christmas approaches and I am acutely aware of the need to cope, to ensure that we are able to celebrate reasonably well as a family.

I take some comfort in verses from Isaiah 43: 'Do not fear for I have redeemed you, *I have summoned you by name; you are mine.* When you pass through the waters, I will be with you; and when you pass through the rivers they will not sweep over you. When you walk through the fire you will not be burned; the flames will not set you ablaze. For I am the Lord your God, the Holy One of Israel, your Saviour.'

The 'not be burned' reminds me of the healing of my side after I tried to burn it off. I remember that I am Peppy. 'God will enlarge the place of your tent'. He continues to show me mercy. My fear subsides somewhat.

I hold onto Isaiah 54:4 too: 'Do not be afraid; you will not be put to shame. Do not fear disgrace; you will not be humiliated. You will forget the shame of your youth…' I know I must choose to see the good that is being brought forward by all this. The treatment of a cancerous tumour is not pleasant, but health can be released by it. The waves of doubt and fear threaten to swamp my raft of faith, and I am often tempted to jump ship and swim ashore.

Today I find myself wandering bleakly through the High Street, buffeted by purposeful Christmas shoppers. I'm not sure what I came here for; I've no idea where I'm going.

I've been avoiding John this last couple of weeks. I'm sure he must be well aware of the changing public perception of me. He may have anticipated it, of course, and I know I cannot really demand sympathy. Once exposed, I cannot expect to veil myself again.

A text message lets me know that he is in the vestry and has time to see me. Once through the door and starting to set my predicament before him, I crumble.

John says that we must re-establish our meetings with Ruth, despite them having tailed into disuse. I am appalled. I begin debating with God – trying to negotiate my way out of facing it. I am in panic and despair that all this has resurrected after months of relative security, peace, and joy.

Out of the blue today, I am reminded of a conversation I had with God, and of what he revealed to me last summer, at a retreat centre where I was involved in a working party. In the chapel, after a time of review, I felt God ask me how much I trusted him. This was pushed to the point where I said yes – yes, I trusted him. Even with your mental health? I agreed that yes, he had already proved sovereign and trustworthy with this, so yes… I did trust him with my mental health. At the time, this seemed a bit odd, after all I'd come through by then. But I took it as part of the review. I wanted to stay humble and keep praising and worshipping God.

Now I am shocked at the reminder of this conversation, at the realisation that God may well be asking me to step into the void again. I am somehow more scared of taking this next part out of the box than all the previous stuff, even though I am also stupefied by what it actually is.

Entering the vestry to meet John and Ruth, I feel acutely uncomfortable. These two know how low I've been, and now I'm aware that there are further depths to probe. How can I bear their repugnance? I feel I am cornered by impending censure.

I'm also fearful of being before this God who sees what sullies my hands even while they are clasped behind my back. I'm afraid of laying the evidence before him and of facing what is due.

John and Ruth ask me to describe what has brought us back

together again. I flounder to articulate that, my mind reeling against committing to any further examination. They appear to me as agents of prosecution. Despite the sham front I have tried to flourish, these two know the reality of my wretchedness and must surely despise me for it – as must God. I can't bear to face any of them.

I can't go on. We close the session in prayer. I am as dismayed as I am relieved.

My sessions with John and Ruth have run into the sand. Every time I meet with them I feel I am in mental freefall. I'm not really in control of this fragile mysterious part of me that's on a frightening tightrope.

I usually manage a good front for others, even though I have the continuing sense of being despised. As people have become aware of my prayer counselling sessions and pick up whispers here and there of what lies behind them, I believe they must think badly of me. I listen to worship music whenever I can to encourage my faith. I take every opportunity to serve in the church and through the various activities I feel worthwhile. Seeing God at work around me trumps any self-loathing flailing around inside me.

Last night I had a very vivid dream. It was set in a city with large sandstone buildings, where I'm walking about trying to find John and Ruth for a meeting, though reluctant about getting there. Things get in my way – objects, people, even the buildings are shifting and sliding into and around each other – making my efforts futile.

I wake, drenched, and when I finally sleep again after a couple of hours, the dream is repeated. This time there is a clock face with hands set at five minutes to the hour. Despite feeling that it's too late, I am compelled to keep searching, jostled and disorientated at every turn. Then I get to a door and I know John and Ruth are on the other side and I know from God that he wants me to go in.

I wake exhausted but at peace.

22: Naming the shame

Journal entries and emails – February to early March of Year 3

The old windows of the vestry have a warped translucence, as though flaccid glass had slightly slumped into itself in the making, obscuring the view in from the outside without any need for nets or blinds.

We review the last week and I tell them about my dream. Mentally, I stand up, bracing myself as a soldier with my armour on, and look at whatever God would have me walk towards.

A picture spreads before me. I stand in a large sandy landscape, fairly barren. While I feel safe where I am, I know that there is an undefined boundary circling me, beyond which there are brown serpents, poisonous snakes, their shapes just visible. Staying where I am gives me a sense of great sadness or loss, even though there is no appeal in the land beyond, yet it feels a place into which I should venture. Will this be 'extending my boundary'?

Then comes a sudden series of pictures, snapshots of moments in my memories. They are milestones of misery from my past that I do not want to see, moments in my life when saying 'no' failed me in some way, led to costly consequences for me. I try to dispel them, to focus on the barren landscape with its strangely tantalising border.

Words of overcoming and endurance from the Bible float as though on ether in the room.

A voice speaks about poisonous snakes that bite at a complaining people who have lost sight of their one true God. I know there are connections – perhaps with Jehoshaphat's story – but cannot quite make them. It's something to do with bad alliances, ungodly treaties and breaking of covenant. I am unsettled by the veiled implications. The weight of my past complicity in depravity drags at my heart. I lurch within, clinging to a trust that God can only be working for my good, but entangled by a swirling fear of banishment.

I am brought out of this dispiriting eddy. John and Ruth reassure me that God is with me and will reveal his purposes at the right time.

Back home, I review the time. I remember Old Testament stories about the service of false gods alienating people from God, and I'm struggling to understand what these thoughts mean. I know I have a new identity in Christ and that God loves me and will not abandon me. I try to cling to my trust in the God who can only be working for my good.

Standing by the paddock fence I watch the crows. Their spiky black forms make distinct nicks in the skyline as they rise and fall in scythe-like arcs. As they settle on the ground they are lost to my eye. I see a connection with the snakes in the desert picture. In both images there is a blending into the landscape that represents something sinister. What is blended into my internal landscape? Why does some of my past remain camouflaged and potentially dangerous?

The sun streams in a rosy gold swathe through the trees on the far side of the field, and I turn and walk towards it.

As I go again through the vestry door, I have to steady myself. I feel fearful, suspicious of John and Ruth's agenda, afraid of their being part of my undoing. I am so deeply afraid of being stripped bare, of being exposed and deemed irredeemable. Yet I have nowhere else to turn.

We begin to pray. I'm desperate for a lifeline but hang in a void. I try to make sense or progress, though this oscillates with my petrified resistance.

The same snapshot pictures are all that flash before me, as though I have looked into a mirror which has cracked apart, the many jagged pieces giving me harsh glimpses of jigsaw memories. I don't want them, they are terribly disquieting. But, apart from the cluttering, flickering parade, there is nothing. I appeal for an image that I can make constructive use of, an image that will provide a way of progress. But I have no more pictures. I am lost in darkness.

I hear Ruth and John's prayers and am pulled to an island of temporary refuge. Stupefied, I make my way home. I am so tired. I have such a headache, and I am jagged and rattled inside. I am so upset... so upset with God.

Too many people at the evening service. I need my own space and sit near the back. The communion elements stick in my throat. Then everyone is suddenly on their feet, moving around, hands extended as the traditional spoken blessing of 'Peace' followed by the words '... be with you' is offered. I feel panic rising. I struggle to cope with people advancing on me, their invading handshakes, unwelcome hugs and kisses. I try to hold myself together at each approach but struggle when I hear the word 'peace' not to respond with '... off'. I thought I'd be fine. I'm frightened by my vulnerability. Michael's arm is around me and leading me away and out.

March 14, 18:43
To: **John; Ruth**
Subject: **today**

I am so pissed off. I feel upset and angry with God for whatever is or isn't going on. If he wants to do business with me, then why not just show me what it is so we can deal with it and not have an excruciating fishing expedition into the murky depths of a past that is dead and buried? What sort of help is this to waste hours locked in a confusing jumble of memory fragments that's nothing to do with my life now or how I can serve him?

Okay, I sank low, prostituting myself in the name of having a semblance of control which, of course, was a complete fallacy. Perhaps it's better to be called a bloody whore and deserve it than it being completely unjustified. That doesn't matter, though. The point is, God wasn't there then but it was all cleaned up once I did find him, I was made okay again. I've been confident in that for ages, so why start to pick that apart in me again?

I can't cope with no pictures. Why stop the pictures when he knows how important they are to me and how I make sense of things? Why leave me stranded?

Two steps back today. What have I got wrong here, because God surely doesn't intend to make me feel like this?

P

Re-reading passages in Exodus in which God reassured the Israelites on their desert journey, I try to come to terms with the fact that while from my perspective things may seem unnecessarily hard, God's purpose is to ensure my future wellbeing. John said to me during the last session that this was about shame, not guilt, but I don't think I understand.

Collecting the post from the porch, I find I have a book which I must have ordered, but don't remember. *The Land Between* by Jeff Manion uses the Israelites' journey through the Sinai desert as a metaphor for being in an undesired transitional place. Transitions, it says, 'provide your greatest opportunity for spiritual growth' and 'God's desire to meet you is most present in these times of chaos and emotional upheaval.' Seems apt. And I feel that if I end up throwing it across the room, the broken spine of a book doesn't matter too much.

23: Shouting the why

Journal entries and emails – Early March of Year 3

I have been poring over the book constantly. My attention is caught by the reminder of how even Moses questioned God, 'Why?' Even *he* had an exhausted rant while battling discouragement. Elijah too had an exasperated emotional meltdown. These are the kind of raw honest prayers that God welcomes from us. What's crucial is the turning towards God, expressing the truth of our experience and opening ourselves to receive his answer.

I also read that what seem to us to be detours on the journey are in fact places where God is waiting to meet us. Understanding that God allows us to experience difficulties, even intense stress and agony, for ultimately redemptive purposes, is key. As the book says, 'God is willing to inflict great pain in order to prevent astronomical pain.'

The wilderness, then, is learning ground. Co-operating, rather than complaining, leads us to transformation.

The thought strikes me that in all the time I sought forgiveness of my past, especially when I first became a Christian, I always fudged the specifics of certain events in my life. I didn't want to name any of what I'd been subject to or, arguably, complicit with. I never have.

This reminds me of a parent and child conversation when the child is in disgrace:

'I'm sorry.'

'What are you sorry for?'

'Being bad.'

'Sorry for... what?'

'Just being bad... I'm sorry for being bad. Oka-aay?'

And I keep my dirty hands out of view, behind my back. I know now that's partly why last week's meeting was so excruciating. I don't want to name my shame. But my loving Father wants me to be completely open and honest before him.

I have become wrung out, fraying, fragile, again finding being with people is too much. I'm despondent at being this way again. I am desperate for God. I'm so pathetic. Please hold me, gentle and mighty God. Catch me when I fall.

Last night I dreamed I was standing in a courtroom box. Everyone was waiting for me to give evidence… and in the quiet thickness of waiting it was clear that they all knew what I should speak about. Court officials moved about, shuffling papers, not looking at me. There was an atmosphere of distaste caused by my sullying presence. When I tried to speak, a ridiculous gibberish dribbled out of my mouth and they cringed. Everyone despised me, and what I could not speak of, and what noises I made. Yet, if I had spoken clearly, we would all have been so appalled and ashamed.

Damned if I do, damned if I don't.

◈ ◈ ◈

April 3, 21:18
To: **John; Ruth**
Subject: **unpacking**

One thing I've had a problem with in the last few weeks is the shouting at God... something that shocks me because it's irreverent and I hadn't realised it was in me. I've been shouting at him, 'Why weren't you *there*? Why didn't you turn up sooner in my life?'

Over the years, I've done a lot of the work of separating myself from what I had been, and getting onto a more stable and healthy footing in life. Then I came to faith. Great! Except now I am struggling with *why not before?* Until recently I've just been happy that finding God happened when it did, that it happened at all. Now I feel slightly cheated and let down because he could have come earlier but didn't. I'm not sure whether I want to shout in outrage or bite my tongue in embarrassment at that. How childish am I!

My first ideas of faith came from two friends. I spent years considering they had something valid but felt I didn't qualify for the club. I didn't actually reject the possibility of God, I simply felt too unworthy to be acceptable. So *why* didn't he break through that before? Too bloody polite? Why wait until I'd been cheated on and felt the sting of lustful betrayal of trust? Was he waiting until I was more acceptable? I don't really believe that, but those feelings keep bubbling up sulphurously. So I'm hurting more now about something that I didn't bother about before, even though it isn't relevant because he's here and loves me and accepts me now. The question of 'why not before?' gnaws away.

This seems all wrong. I thought I was going to be okay when I walked out of the vestry. Why is it so tenuous? It seems that the woman at the well and the woman caught in adultery were healed and dashed off brightly to tell everyone how great Jesus was. I feel I'd be two-faced to consider doing that right now. It seems every time I submit to exposing a difficult area I then discover it's a bigger and more hostile area than I'd realised. Actually, I'm afraid that I'm going to let God down and not manage to get to a properly healed place after all.

I'm sorry, both of you. I need to articulate this even though it's not what any of us want to hear. I will keep trying.

Peppy

I spend an unsettled night thinking about alliances. I didn't enter into bad alliances in the past because it was appealing or beneficial to me. Quite the opposite. But I was acting as though that was the deal, and the stakes got higher and higher, the more I engaged with that. It was a sham. Like quicksand. If you lie still you'll keep your head above it for longer. If you struggle, you'll be consumed in the mire in no time.

I feel I'm being punished for entering into that mentality even though it was a matter of self-preservation. If I wanted it, was gratified by it, that would be reasonable. But this is so unfair.

But then I realise… I've been afraid that if I open up and give over all my secret horrid stuff to God, I risk losing my mental health. In fact, God is showing me that *if I don't*, I will lose my mental health. The paranoia I've sometimes experienced is a warning… that's the poisonous snakes. And the crows? The gifts God has given me will be stolen if I don't act to get rid of the crows.

This revelation gives me a new road to walk, even though I don't know the steps to take.

24: Describing the snapshot

Journal entries – March of Year 3

Another Easter and another Easter stations event at a local primary school, and again I'm helping Ruth and John. This year, our presentation of the Easter story hinges on paintings, particularly two well known paintings – Da Vinci's 'Last Supper' and 'Supper at Emmaus' by Caravaggio. This second one depicts the moment when the true identity of Jesus is revealed to two of his companions following his death.

With all the children sitting expectantly in the main hall, John begins by relating the story of Easter from the Bible. Ruth takes over, using pictures on the projector screen, describing how pictures can tell stories. On the screen we see Jesus returning to Jerusalem on Palm Sunday. The people are cheering, waving palm leaves, greeting Jesus as the one to save them from the oppressive Roman occupation. Yet he rides a donkey as a sign of peace.

Another picture shows the angry outburst of Jesus in the Temple, reacting to the way people treat the holy place like a marketplace. His red cloak is pointed out as a visual clue to that anger.

Now the scene of the Last Supper fills the screen. Where is your eye drawn? Ruth asks the children. What does the artist want us to notice? 'Yes, that's right,' she nods at a child who has volunteered the answer. Jesus is at the centre. We notice the halo effect created by the window behind him. His arms are wide. He is still, while around him there is agitation.

Why are all the people in the painting on only one side of the table? That's right! The observer is being invited in, being included, allowed to be part of what is happening. Ruth encourages the children to be detectives. What clues can they find in the painting? Aha! Judas is holding a money bag, showing that he is about to 'sell out'. Other disciples reveal their emotions. James is angry, shocked. Philip seems wistful or bewildered. The children are directed to Judas. He is not painted as the archetypal 'baddie'. The children think he looks a little absent-minded. Perhaps a bit dim. Perhaps sad. Perhaps a little disappointed in Jesus.

After a break in the playground, the children are ready to settle to what comes next. John talks them through the events in the Garden of Gethsemane, the arrest, the fake trial and then the terrible death and the first glimpse of Jesus risen from death.

Ruth's turn again. The screen shows the Caravaggio painting. So, people were sad, disappointed, bewildered because Jesus was dead. Two followers are walking away from Jerusalem, devastated by the whole turn of events. All is lost. The hoped-for Messiah has been executed like a common criminal.

Ruth describes how the two are joined by a stranger who questions their downcast mood. The stranger begins to explain the Scriptures to them, showing how Jesus has fulfilled prophecies. They invite him to share a meal and stay the night. As the man breaks the bread, they suddenly realise who he is. Jesus is alive – and he is with them!

'Where is your eye drawn this time?' asks Ruth. The children identify that again the focus is Jesus, the lines of perspective and light falling on his face. The shadow on the wall creates a dark halo behind his head as if to portray the darkness of the cross that lies behind him. Light from an unseen window illumines his face from one side. Fruit in a bowl on the table is both withered and ripe – depicting death and decay and life all together. Jesus is unexpectedly clean-shaven, almost boyish – perhaps renewed; certainly not ravaged by thorns, the ripping whip and the puncturing nails and spear. The outstretched arms of one of the men at the table recall the crucifixion pose as he exclaims in revelation. He wears a shell on his tabard, the sign of a pilgrim or seeker. They have found Jesus in that moment and everything is transformed.

There is such dynamic in this freeze-framed moment, so much to discover within it, so much revealed when you simply describe the snapshot.

The children return to their classrooms. Time stands still for me. I know that's my next step. Tell the story… describe the snapshot. Describe the snapshot. This is what God wants me to do.

I am submitting to the inevitable, though feeling desperate to resist. John and Ruth are here in the vestry, though I cannot focus on them. The import of this place and this time looms over and around me, obscuring all else.

Words of prayer skim the air. I have my list… the list of those snapshot pictures. I just need to get on with it, though the prospect is appalling. Yet self-disembowelling is no less welcome than containing the rot within.

Yes, I have my list. I hold it up in my hand through the waves of panic, like polluting flotsam. I begin to name the images on each picture that has been flashed before me.

Tell the story. Describe the snapshot. I name each chapter. I speak the detail. These are the significant moments in my life where the word 'no' failed me. The consequences of each hang heavy in my conscience. The cost of each is great. The cumulative evidence of guilt against me seems beyond both doubt and redemption, but I offer these moments up regardless.

I come to the last piece, the most jagged and piercing one of all… the one that brings such utter degradation into piercingly sharp relief. Having felt so actively complicit and apparently lurid in attitude in that relationship, gossip spread. I had gained a certain reputation, though I didn't feel entitled to any respect I'd lost. Some time later, this in itself exposed me to a further danger, stripping away the last remnant of any perceived right to object or complain about anyone taking advantage of my body. This time two men – smirking – locked a door behind us and, indifferent to my dissent, spent time enacting and imposing their perverted fantasies into my reality. I was mute, utterly shocked and traumatised by this rape.

This was an abomination. My self-abhorrence was complete. As time went on, I shut it away. Not even God should be allowed to look upon this horrific dark corner of my life.

This then, is the last snapshot… this trauma, this time when the terrified no that was screaming within me was betrayed by my inert tongue. The intimate intrusion of this degradation took any last vestige of dignity. This piece has never been held in any light before but is surely the conclusive condemnation of my true self. I am overwhelmed and alone in a black void. My soul cries out, a desperate distress flare arcing out from the depths of this awful chasm.

Snap! Snap!

His face is momentarily before me. I am caused to look up at it, to gaze in fearful awe at this omniscient visage. I am shocked by love.

A moment later, there's a sense of breaking, a crack deep within me.

His face! It is the face of Jesus before me… a face of still and striking beauty looking straight at me, looking into me, penetrating my being.

The crack creates a fissure where his love flows in. It binds onto my shame and claims it as his own. My burden is gone. He tenderly upholds me. The potential he has invested in me far outweighs any loss that life has dealt.

My old narrative is overlaid by the redeeming and perpetual story of transforming love. I am pulled out of the ocean pit and lie exhausted on the life-raft that has been cast my way.

The Chronicles of the Box

Part 3

25: Aftershocks

Emails and journal entries – March to August of Year 3

March 20, 18:08
To: **John; Ruth**
Subject: **unpacking session**

Thank you so much for staying alongside me today, as well as all the other days. I feel a bit strange at the moment – relieved, grateful, exhausted, overwhelmed by this new perspective on God's love for me, unworthy but accepting.

I have an image of a newly split chrysalis, a still wet and crumpled butterfly beside it hanging onto the branch. It's a new creation, but must rest and wait for the blood to pump up its wings before it can fly, before the full beauty of what God has reformed of this creature can be appreciated. It is a new creation, but is only so because of how it once was and how the process of change worked.

I feel tired out by the struggle of emergence. It was too dark inside the chrysalis but now I can see what's happening to me and I'm in awe. But it's too early to show off those wings yet.

For now, I am quiet, with a sense of wonder at what has been done, and what it will mean in time to come.

I accepted your hugs before I left because I thought if I didn't that a remnant of 'Am I despised?' could have taken hold again, and I'm so determined not to let it govern me again. Maybe that awareness tells me I will need a certain vigilance as I move forward, that a full healing may need more time and care. But I sensed nothing in either of you that communicated unease or revulsion of me, which is enormously helpful. I'm sure that whatever I need to plump up my wings now, God will guide me with, as and when necessary. I know God's working really hard in me, and I have a responsibility to work with him, and I will.

Quite why God loves me, all of me, is beyond me. But I have a better grasp today that he does.

Thank you again and again, my precious companions on the way.

Love and blessings to you both,

Peppy

Time out is good, and healing too. We watch a DVD as a family, sprawling on our outsized sofa, all tangled limbs and cushioning torsos. We share a giant bottle of cloudy lemonade and assorted snacks. It's *The King's Speech*. I realise that Bertie was a 'wounded speaker' and that he always had his impediment to struggle with, it was never easy or comfortable. But while his speech therapist Lionel was close, he was able to deliver speeches that were important to the nation's morale during the wartime.

Later that week, recognising the need for it, Michael and I cancel some commitments to visit a couple of stately homes. We wander hand in hand around the exhibits. Outside we run around the garden features and our fun together brings out smiles that we realise we've lacked in recent weeks.

August 9, 06:16
To: **John; Ruth**
Subject: **unpacking**

This can't wait... Today is the third day that I have woken up 'not mental', and finally knowing that something has changed in me. The joy I have in that is beautiful.

Yesterday there was the most spectacular rainbow over the village that my lovely daughter and I just thrilled over. We stopped the car on the hill so she could take pictures on her phone, and I rejoiced to be reminded with a deeper faith and understanding now that God's word and promises are utterly dependable, and his saving grace is awesome. He loves me unconditionally, for who he created me to be, and he has a plan and purpose for my life centred on him. How wonderful (full of wonder!) is that!

Love and blessings to you both,

Peppy x

At a conference on the subject of reconciling storytelling, I am thinking more deeply about forgiveness. I am reminded repeatedly that we are people with the capacity for doing awful things and making bad choices.

I am struck by the words of a well-known worker for justice Clive Stafford Smith insisting 'you cannot define a person by the worst fifteen minutes of their life'. I become aware that I have demonised several people for their wrong acts against me – but God looks on them with compassion and sees them in balance, in entirety. Although they had become monsters in my mind, there is more to them than my memories allow for. I need to ask God to help me see them more as he does, to help me continue forgiving them.

At a festival of faith, justice and arts, I hear talks given by Erwin James – an ex-lifer who found redemptive change through the opportunities opened up by education and writing. He is now a free man, now serving the good of prisoners. Hearing him speak about his life, I contemplate how, with the right care and support, even hard-as-stone criminals may discover hearts of flesh.

I am particularly impacted by a talk given at the same event by Sara Hyde. Sara speaks of a secure and happy upbringing, and how her understanding of those around her is shaken by the utterly shocking and unexpected sexual assault of one friend by another. It leads to her devoting her working life to the criminal justice system and advocacy, to changing lives and perception.

I come out of the room reeling… humbled and shaken … realising that we simply cannot box people up simplistically in good or bad terms. We all have goodness within us, and we all have wrongdoing potentially perpetually present. We are all capable of change. We may choose to champion a good way for others. God is challenging me to re-frame my perceptions of those who hurt me… and it's not an easy task to engage in.

These experiences help me further accept that good or ordinary people can choose to do bad things, but that doesn't wholly define them or mean they are beyond redemption or out of God's love. Yes, there will be an accounting for all our wrongdoings, but maybe there is more to God's response than justice alone.

Reflecting further, I see how the bad things people did to me actually came out of their own brokenness and woundedness. Those who abused me were informed by exposure to and involvement in harmful influences such as damage from hard porn. One was himself abused by parents. They practiced selfishness and misogyny, normalising their right to take what they wanted from someone over whom they could exert power. As for those who were silent, who looked away – my mother, and perhaps others – they have something broken in them that I don't understand. I suppose a part of me still grieves for a 'mum'. I wonder about what hidden brokenness is there in the withdrawal and silence shown by her and others that I have not yet been shown or entrusted with. But that is between them and God. My aim is to honour my mother unconditionally with no expectation of any return. I believe God will enable me to do that.

We are all broken, all prone to sin, all needing God's forgiveness and healing. There's good and evil in each one of us. Every time God responds in love and mercy to our brokenness, it's unmerited and totally wonderful. It's better for me to look at myself and not think of 'grading' another person's sin or looking for penalty for them. God can be trusted with perfect justice – alongside his loving mercy.

26: Safely home

Postcript

The months pass. It's not an entirely smooth path, but I feel steadily stronger. I know that there is no place for triumphalism here, but that reverence and gratitude are the pastures that ongoing dependency grazes on.

The aftershocks continue. God holds me safe. I feel like he has glued the pieces together, but the glue hasn't yet dried so I have to be very careful and not move much. I try to stay still in his hands. Just waiting. I'm aware of how different an outcome there would have been without God's presence and action, and that sobers me.

In the waves of emotional backwash, I sometimes want not to continue working through all this. But knowing God is with me enables me to resolve to lift my eyes. And then there is the family… without them, I could so easily opt out.

This phase has been harder, riskier than I imagined it could be. At times I have felt in danger of completely losing my mental health. I remember that God showed me that if I did *not* go through the healing process, then I would indeed lose it. I have been kept safe.

The challenges continue. The internal processes are at times hard and painful. God has healed me and is healing me – but there was no 'magic wand' moment. He healed me *just enough* so that I could open up and keep working through layer upon layer with him. To do otherwise may have irreparably damaged me. I am humbled by God's gentle wisdom in this. The shards have not been discarded but transformed into a mosaic, a beautiful testament to his restoration and healing. God has respected all that has made me *me*… and he has used it with a new and enlarged sense of purpose.

'A man cannot be led out of the desert by one who has never been there,' says Henri Nouwen. I believe that now I have something important to share; an insight and empathy into other people's experiences of abuse. It takes courage to address these things, but it is absolutely worthwhile.

Much has been lost now from my life. The hidden fear and shame, the suppressed rage – these have dissipated and given way to a new and deep sense of peace and security. I understand now that shame is about who I am, not what I've done. Confession releases guilt, but it's not that way for shame. Shame carries with it a fear of rejection if you confess. I had felt I must, I must, be silent. But that harmful bond is now broken.

Other things have changed. Four years of neurological symptoms – tingling, numbness and loss of fine motor skills on my left side – have ceased. Intermittent drenching night sweats have stopped. The negative inner dialogue that had always accompanied times of intimacy has fallen silent. The freshness and freedom of mind and body have been a revelation.

The cost to me of what God has asked these last few years is nothing compared to the cost he paid for me on the cross. I am worth that to him. I have been through despair and distress, I have found where my hope is, and have experienced the healing and renewal that only God has the power to give.

My name is Peppy. I have been called by name. I will tell of his love.

I have completed training as a Christian listener, a skill that will help me to be alongside and listen to others as they tell their stories. It's not a way of intervening with what they need to have heard; it's a way to help them better understand their own feelings about a situation, and then discover their own way forward. It's a tool that seems to fit naturally in my hand, one that I know will help me serve God and others with wisdom and sensitivity.

I have new courage in speaking out. We work through discussions on sexuality at church and I feel I can speak out against abusive relationships. My concern is not about defining 'right' or 'wrong' kinds of sexualities, but commending relationships of real love of any kind. I want to defend those experiencing shame or the bonds of unhealthy relationships – as I know how destructive those things can be. I choose to be open – a bit of 'outing' that brings a backwash. But the insecurity over that passes. I also contribute to a talk about divorce and the breaking of bonds.

I'm not sure the scars will ever go away and that's fine. I have learned about kintsugi, the Japanese art of broken pots. The pots are mended with lacquer dusted or mixed with powdered gold, silver, or platinum. The result is that the scars are beautifully highlighted, rather than hidden. Brokenness can be part of beauty.

I know that the purging period I have been through and the raw edges this has left in me allows God to work through me more effectively. I know that what God enables me to do for him remains founded on my human fragility. I am deeply grateful.

Dani and I work together occasionally, creating reflective, interactive displays in our church which the public can spend time with, hopefully seeing something of God's love in their lives. Three years on from the Easter in which I told my story to the church family, we create a display called 'God in the Gardens'. We intertwine Eden, Gethsemane and the garden tomb of the resurrected Jesus. Through an installation of artwork, pottery, words, fresh flowers and greenery, we try to show how God is present and meets us in our brokenness, bringing redemption and new life. Sitting in the pews, watching discreetly from the back of the church, I love to watch God at work as people pause to look long, taking it all in.

I have been away on a silent retreat. Eight days in a rambling old house with nothing to do but the hard work of doing business with God. The space serves to show me that sometimes I still retain a reluctance to allow the Father too close. I am astonished and irked by this, and wrestle with it all week. And then in prayer I am given a most amazing picture.

Nestled in a stack of large cushions in the low dappled light of a basement chapel, I focus on imagining being 'at home' with Jesus. I have been asked to try to allow him to bring his Father in too.

As I imagine this, the room becomes similar to my home. It is open plan, as it has been since the dividing wall was removed. The split level lounge allows a view through the dining room and across the end of the kitchen. The freestanding wooden units fill one wall of the dining room and surround the kitchen sink unit.

I am sitting low on the floor of the lounge. I am observing Jesus and his Father moving around in my kitchen, going about in ordinary domesticity – clearing and cleaning and communing. They are utterly attuned to each other, sharing a great regard. There is an obvious joy and delight between them. They have not looked at me, but I know they know I am here, and they are quietly pleased about that.

I then have a thought about how I am placed in the lounge, watching them but slightly separate, as an observer. I find I wish I could be closer.

Suddenly they are sitting, legs tucked under, either side and facing me. I am honoured, yet slightly awed and awkward. I pray for the grace to stay with this picture.

There is such gentle respect and care here. I am astonished when each one picks up one of my legs. I am momentarily aware of a particular vulnerability and indignity in this position.

'Relax, we've got you,' I sense from the One.

'I made you, remember?' I understand from my Creator.

Now my feet are being washed over a large white china bowl that has a golden interior. They each soap my feet, working in and around the toes and massaging my soles and heels. It is an awesome sensation. They seem to have pleasure and satisfaction in doing this.

They dip my feet into the bowl of water, then lift them up again to have fresh water from a jug poured over. My feet are lowered onto a fluffy white towel which is now spread between them, so that my feet now rest on each of their knees, being patted and pressed dry.

My feet are lowered onto the floor between them, still on the outspread towel.

Each leans on one arm, while remaining sitting with me. There is a deep pleasure between us, and deep gratitude from me to them. And great love.

I tell them, 'I love this! Thank you! Thank you!'

We remain together, content, in companionship. There is no need to leave this place. The house is mine, but now his. It is a safe house, where I am loved.

The Chronicles of the Box

Part 4

27: Easter revisited

This book has been several years in the writing. On many occasions I have thought that I had reached a kind of conclusion, a plateau or place where a line could be drawn under the hard graft of change. I have learned that's not possible. Following each breakthrough there have been more trials… even, dare I say it, other forms of abuse. God has made me different and sometimes other people find that mystifying, challenging. Sometimes people want to put me straight and don't understand God has called me to a path that's full of diversions. Moving on from victimhood, ironically, can cause others to feel unsettled or threatened. My becoming creative, with a growing confidence and independence, has been welcomed and celebrated by many. But, for a few, it's upsetting to the status quo and may be resented. Those making different choices for dealing with sensitive issues can be affronted and challenged by someone who grasps the nettle and is open about it.

I am deeply grateful and have absolutely no regrets about dealing with my past as I did. I had to, really. But there has been great cost, too. And not just to myself. The choices I made, in prospect and legacy, impacted others in deep ways that may take a great deal of working through. For that, I sorrow. A great deal of care is needed in dealing with such deep issues, even with God's help, as the effects on those exposed to the traumas can be insidious and profound without the right preparation or aftercare. May we come to see the good purpose out of the extended mess we so naively entered into, yet still trust God to have charge. The story is not over yet.

Easter is always being revisited. I am often drawn to think about the days following Jesus' death, and the new work of the Holy Spirit in the world that was revealed then.

Jesus kept moving… the cross became empty, the tomb became empty. In his appearances, he moved further and further away from the places where the 'old' things had ended. He had to move to lead people to the new things coming, but he could only move to the new from the real and tangible foundations of the old.

Those around him, who loved and respected him, would have felt shocked and appalled at the brutish way Jesus had died. They surely felt some incredulity and lack of readiness to take the mission forward. But what seemed like a situation of loss, destruction and pointlessness became a new time of God's power, renewal and purpose.

Those disciples had to be a bridge – taking all their experience of their time lived alongside Jesus, all he had taught them then, and how the Spirit was leading them on to do their part in taking the gospel out into the world. They were the connection between the old physical experiences with Jesus and the new covenant and blessing through the power of the Holy Spirit being made available for all. They could witness from the vantage point of having been there through the transition from the old to the new, knowing that both matter.

I visit Coventry Cathedral. The old cathedral was destroyed by incendiary bombs during the Second World War. The immediate response by the church was to make a statement of forgiveness in the way they rebuilt. This would have been shocking, appalling and unexpected to most people, given that it was early on in the war and people would not have felt naturally inclined or ready to respond with forgiveness. Yet there was a choice to move forward in a spirit of grace and forgiveness. When the new cathedral was built, it remained connected to the old ruins, and a significant ministry of forgiveness and reconciliation was built from that.

Inside the new cathedral I am struck that when someone has received communion at the altar rail, the first thing they then do is to turn and walk back towards the world, with the old ruins in sight. They are literally looking at, and being reminded of, the remains of the old building and all that that represents. I recall the clutter of Jerusalem – built, razed and rebuilt over time – where the layers remain exposed in places. That foundational rubble is intrinsic to its purpose too. God embraces it all. He does not obliterate all that is old and past, but renews and builds good things from it. We are not to stay static. We are to be his disciples moving out and away into the world, however he wills that to happen. Each time God moves me in some way I feel unready or inadequate, and have to keep re-learning the pattern of following him in faith. I'm honoured to keep doing that, to know myself redeemed, to keep finding my way from pain and wilderness to resurrection.

John:

The day I first met Penny in our church coffee shop, she was discussing her puppeteering with a friend. Not being one to miss an opportunity, I invited them to bring their puppets to my church's holiday club the following year. They did – and it was a huge success.

Several years passed, and Penny and her family eventually began to attend my church regularly. Together we developed Basil Brush-style puppet assemblies to take around local schools once a term.

Because she used British Sign Language during the worship in services, Penny was known in our church as 'the lady that signs, not sings'. But I also remember someone describing her as 'precious Penny'. I was aware that there was a fragile edge to her.

One day she asked if she could see me, I think to ask some question about forgiveness, and in the New Year 2011 we met up. In time, she described to me her 'visions of the box'. Sketchily, she outlined the bad situation she'd been in as a child with her stepfather. And she described how some years later she'd felt compelled to tell the story to the police, in case the man was still a risk to children. In the event, it turned out that he had died some years before, and Penny was released from telling the rest of the story at that point. How it came about that she did tell the rest of the story is the theme of this book.

I am no expert on spiritual, inner or emotional healing but, in the land of the blind, the man with one eye is king! I have a personal passion for it because I long to see people freed, whole and joyful before God. Experiences earlier in my life had taught me three things. Firstly, God heals. No, really! Physically, emotionally, spiritually... God really does heal people. Secondly, this is tricky territory and one should not sally forth where angels fear to tread. Happily, my own experiences had not only taught me something about *how* to do it but – perhaps more importantly – how *not* to do it. The theology of this is not simple or straightforward because, irritatingly, God doesn't do what we tell him! God directs and decides the process and the onus is on us to accept the outcome.

Thirdly, if God doesn't heal, healing doesn't happen.

So my role, and that of my co-counsellor Ruth, was to provide a safe environment where Penny could meet God and God could work. It wasn't a 'system'; we didn't use 'magic' phrases, but there were some guidelines.

Any healing prayer is a story about God. It's about God's grace, mercy and power in the life of an individual, redeeming the past and releasing them for a future of service. Importantly, unless Penny was serious about engaging with God and getting closer to him, no amount of prayer on our part was going to make a jot of difference. God is courteous and will not override someone's willingness to surrender. This isn't about someone being freed from the bad stuff to live an easy, comfortable life without God. God cares too much about anyone to let them do that. This is about being freed to serve, about adopting the role of the wounded healer, about taking up the cross, about sharing in the sufferings of Christ. Ruth and I came alongside and watched as Penny wrestled with her past, wrestled with God and then broke through to new levels of release and realisation of God's unmerited kindly regard on her soul. We held the space; God worked; Penny surrendered. By the end we had all gained a new sense of wonder of God's love. Penny was no more, and Peppy was a new person.

Ruth:

Christ's resurrection features prominently in Peppy's story. My own involvement with her began one Eastertime. Penny and I were sitting in a busy school staffroom after leading some sessions with the children about the meaning of Easter. Somehow we got talking about close relationships. Out of the blue, Penny expressed some hurt and I wasn't quite sure how to respond. What on earth was the right thing to say? People who think that ministers have a book of 'helpful phrases' or special pastoral powers have most definitely got it wrong! Inside, we're often saying a hurried prayer for God to 'help me quick'. I think I floundered a bit before saying something like, 'We can't always keep getting hurt. Sometimes a bit of self-preservation is okay.' Whatever was said, or maybe it was the stuff that wasn't said, it was enough.

The following week John phoned and asked if I'd be interested in helping with some 'prayer ministry' with Penny. This was a phrase I'd come across before and associated with churches that put a lot of pressure on individuals to conform to the expectations of their leadership. I thought the dangers of manipulation were great. Surely professional counselling would be better? Prayer ministry was outside my church tradition and my personal experience – and to say I was wary is a gross understatement.

So what made me agree? One reason was the friendship I had with John. We were two non-conformist ministers in the same small town with churches that got on well together. We had already worked together on number of projects over the years and sorted out some knotty pastoral problems. He didn't strike me as the spiritually bullying type. I was also encouraged by the way John described the process. The idea was not to replace or undermine any future counselling but simply to pray for what Penny wanted us to pray for. The instruction was 'bottom up' rather than 'top down'. In a way, it was no different from Sunday intercessions where we pray for people's physical healing without any expectation that they will abandon the doctor's surgery.

There was something else that persuaded me to agree to be part of this… some prompting that said God was at work here and it would be a privilege to be part of it.

I learned a great deal over the weeks and months that followed. Interestingly, it was learning where I was not 'doing' anything but simply praying and listening for the prompting of the Spirit. My ministry has tended to have an 'activist' shape, so this was something quite different.

I learned just how cruel some people can be. I can remember raging on Penny's behalf about the injustice she'd suffered. I think I even swore. I learned just how brave some people can be in choosing to face their fears and shadows from the past. Above all, I saw the goodness of God: a God who hears, a God who heals, a God who slowly and – yes – painfully at times, leads us into newness of life which brings us to Easter.

Psalm 27 (NIV UK)

The LORD is my light and my salvation –
  whom shall I fear?
The LORD is the stronghold of my life –
  of whom shall I be afraid?

When the wicked advance against me
  to devour me,
it is my enemies and my foes
  who will stumble and fall.
Though an army besiege me,
  my heart will not fear;
though war break out against me,
  even then I will be confident.

One thing I ask from the LORD,
  this only do I seek:
that I may dwell in the house of the Lord
  all the days of my life,
to gaze on the beauty of the LORD
  and to seek him in his temple.
For in the day of trouble
  he will keep me safe in his dwelling;
he will hide me in the shelter of his sacred tent
  and set me high upon a rock.

Then my head will be exalted
  above the enemies who surround me;
at his sacred tent I will sacrifice with shouts of joy;
  I will sing and make music to the LORD.

Hear my voice when I call, LORD;
be merciful to me and answer me.
My heart says of you, 'Seek his face!'
Your face, LORD, I will seek.
Do not hide your face from me,
do not turn your servant away in anger;
you have been my helper.
Do not reject me or forsake me,
God my Saviour.
Though my father and mother forsake me,
the LORD will receive me.
Teach me your way, Lord;
lead me in a straight path
because of my oppressors.
Do not hand me over to the desire of my foes,
for false witnesses rise up against me,
spouting malicious accusations.
I remain confident of this:
I will see the goodness of the LORD
in the land of the living.
Wait for the LORD;
be strong and take heart
and wait for the LORD.

Where to go for help...

acornchristian.org – Acorn Christian organisation, offering listening, training and resources for personal healing and wholeness.

intothelight.org.uk – therapeutic charity, counselling and working with survivors of sexual abuse.

rapecrisis.org.uk – dealing with so-called 'historic' as well as immediate issues around sexual assault; look on the website to find the phone number for your nearest centre.

oneinfour.org.uk – supporting people who've experienced child sexual abuse and trauma.

napac.org – running a support phone line and support groups; tel: 0808 801 0331.

samaritans.org – UK charity offering support via a telephone helpline to people who are suicidal or despairing; on hand 24 hours a day, every day of the year.

nspcc.org.uk – leading children's charity fighting to end child abuse in the UK and Channel Islands.